TIME MANAGEMENT:

50 Lessons on Finding Time for What's Important

Joe Serio, Ph.D.

Project Manager: Jennifer Bailey
Design Team: Harriet McHale, Jena Rodriguez, and Tracey Neikirk

For information, contact GTN Media at info@gtnmedia.com

Printed in the United States of America
ISBN 13: 978-0-9900216-4-3

www.joeserio.com

Contents

The long span of the bridge of your life is supported by countless cables called habits, attitudes, and desires. What you do in life depends upon what you are and what you want. What you get from life depends upon how much you want it, how much you are willing to work and plan and cooperate and use your resources. The long span of the bridge of your life is supported by countless cables that you are spinning now, and that is why today is such an important day. Make the cables strong!

~ L.G. Elliott

About the *Get the Nerve*™ *Series*

The idea for the *Get the Nerve*™ *Series* grew out of my personal transformation from being fearful of most things to facing that fear and achieving more than I thought possible.

My goal is to share what I have learned so that you, too, can see the possibility for your own life and make it a reality.

Each book in the series begins with reflections on fear. This builds the foundation for the following lessons, which are specific to the topic of each book. As L.G. Elliott says in the quotation on the facing page, "Your life is supported by countless cables called habits, attitudes, and desires." This series is a blueprint for helping you create and strengthen the cables of your bridge, so you can live the most inspired life you can imagine.

I would love to hear about changes you make in your life as a result of the *Get the Nerve*™ *Series*. Please contact me with your stories of personal transformation at drjoe@joeserio.com.

Other Titles in the
Get the Nerve™ Series

Introduction

For usually and fitly, the presence of an introduction
is held to imply that there is something of
consequence and importance to be introduced.

~ Arthur Machen

It's really shocking how much time slips through our fingers. Days turn into weeks and months turn into years. We wake up one day wondering where it all went. And still we struggle to figure out how to manage our time better.

We often resign ourselves to spinning on the hamster wheel of life, figuring that that's just the way it is and has to be.

At the same time, we lament about how busy we are while rarely ever questioning if we're chasing the right things.

- Are we adding value to our days?
- Are we chasing things that are meaningless?
- Are we spending our time on things out of guilt or peer pressure?
- Are we saying yes because we don't know how to say no?
- Are we stuck living in a land of "ought to," "should," and "must," rather than "want to" and "love to"?

The impact that poor time management has on our lives is staggering. You feel it yourself day in and day out. It comes in the form of frustration, aggravation, and exhaustion. You often don't get nearly the amount of work done that you planned to; your to-do list is usually mocking you at the end of your day, showing how many things are left undone.

The statistics about the ravages of poor time management are endless. Here are just a few:

- We spend one year of our lives looking for lost or misplaced items.

- Office workers waste up to 30% of their workday.

- Workers lose 7 weeks a year seeking clarification due to poor communication.

- People who multitask decrease their productivity by 20-40% and are less efficient than those who focus on one project at a time.

- Sales representatives are most productive when they assign themselves only three tasks per day.

- It almost always takes twice as long to complete a task as what we originally thought it would take.

It's time for a change. It's time for you to get more out of life. But, the sad fact of the matter is you probably were never taught very much about how to set priorities and create meaningful goals. You weren't taught about productivity and managing your time. You just did what the rest of us did: inherited your parents' habits, watched your colleagues, and made up your own ways, thinking that that's the best way to do it.

Fortunately, there are other ways to get what you want.

How to Use This Book

Time Management: 50 Lessons on Finding Time for What's Important is a practical guide of tools and techniques to help you develop your own system for managing time.

This book is arranged in five parts:

Part 1, Fear, provides context for the book and helps create a mindset you'll use to dramatically improve your time management. It is the foundation for the remainder of the book.

Part 2, Goals, lays out the indispensable ingredients needed to set and reach your goals. When you set real goals following the outline in this part of the book, the hardest part of reaching your goals will already be done.

Part 3, System, shows how to effectively manage your day and your things. Simple tools and techniques are at your disposal to help you create more productive and satisfying days with less stress and frustration.

Part 4, Discipline, provides insights and exercises to help you stay on track, say no to the countless requests for your time, and minimize distractions as you go through your day.

Part 5, Going Forward, rounds out the book with a great blueprint for getting what you want and a wonderful success story about what's possible.

While you could read *Time Management* in any order, I recommend reading it from beginning to end. There is an arc, a logical progression, to the lessons.

The benefits you will get from reading — and applying — the lessons in this book cannot be fully described. You must experience it. You will see shifts you never thought possible. You will gain perspective you've never had. You will notice improvement in virtually every area of your life. But it's up to you. No one else can do it for you.

In a nutshell, this book is about you. Everything you need to know to start on your road to better time management is inside you. The tools and techniques I've laid out will help you bring those things out. If you find this process easy, you're probably not doing it right. You will have to ask some difficult questions of yourself and face some painful realities. That's ok. That's normal. But the work is doable, and it's worth it.

Master the lessons in this book and you will gain clarity about what's important to you and how to get more of it. Your life will change and the future will be brighter when you put into practice the kinds of recommendations presented throughout the book.

Part 1

Fear

Lesson 1

The Myth of Time Management

After all is said and done, more is said than done.

~ Aesop

Time is a created thing. To say 'I don't have time,' is like saying, 'I don't want to.'

~ Lao Tzu

If you're like most people, you may think you have a time management problem.

You may frequently find yourself saying, "I'm too busy!" "I don't have enough time!" "I can't get everything done!" "I need more hours in a day!"

I bet you often find yourself in that position, racing around, trying to get everything done, feeling like you can never catch up because there just isn't enough time. You've convinced yourself that you have bad time management skills.

There's one important myth to dispel at the very outset of this book: there is no such thing as time management.

The phrase "time management" is convenient shorthand we all use, but if we're going to get to the heart of the matter, let's be crystal clear about the following fact:

You don't have a time management problem, you have a *self-management* problem.

Time management is really about how you manage your energy; how you set priorities and goals; how well you stick to the plan and adapt to changing circumstances; what you do in the face of distractions; and, perhaps most fundamentally, if you're really chasing the right things. It's about how you manage yourself, not the number of hours in a day.

Everyone gets the same 24 hours allotted each day. Some people get a lot done; others talk a lot about what they're going to do. Some get all of the right things done; others spin their wheels chasing the wrong things. Some keep working toward their goals day in and day out; others get discouraged and quit.

So many people lose massive amounts of time by starting and stopping, shifting gears and changing directions, and finally giving up, never really achieving a fraction of their potential. Is that you?

Here's a basic, easy-to-remember equation summarizing time management:

Time Management = Goals + System + Discipline

There are three questions you can ask yourself to determine whether you're on the right path: 1) Do I have goals that align with my beliefs, values, and priorities? 2) Do I have an effective system for reaching those goals? 3) Am I following that system?

In its simplest terms, this book is about helping you answer those three questions.

At the outset of this journey, you need to summon the courage to look the facts of your self-management in the face: Have you fallen into the trap of believing the myth of time management and complain about how little time there is? Or, do you realize that you don't get enough of the right things done simply because you don't manage yourself well enough?

It's possible you've never made the distinction between "time management" and "self-management." Once you come to terms with it, you'll be in a much better position to look at your tasks differently and put in place ways to get more out of life.

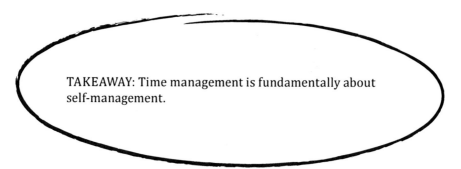

TAKEAWAY: Time management is fundamentally about self-management.

Time Management as a Spiritual Exercise

Tell me, what is it you plan to do with your one wild and precious life?

~ Mary Oliver

Unfortunately, the clock is ticking, the hours are going by. The past increases, the future recedes. Possibilities decreasing, regrets mounting.

~ Haruki Murakami

When I tell my audiences that time management is a spiritual exercise, they usually look at me like, "What's this guy talking about?! Spiritual? I've never heard that before!"

The simple fact of the matter is time is finite. It will run out. Your one short life will be over. Are you using the talents, gifts, and opportunities given to you?

This idea about the finite nature of time was introduced to me when I was around 13 years old. In our church community there was an old Irish priest with a brogue so heavy I could barely understand what he said.

What I managed to decipher turned out to be his main message, one he repeated often, from the Gospel of Matthew: "You do not know the hour or the day." And it's true. It could be tomorrow; it could be when you're in your 90s.

If you ever lose sight of this, simply open a newspaper, turn on the television, or get on the internet on any given day to see countless stories about people's "untimely" deaths. It's a reminder that life is tenuous and precarious, fleeting and precious.

One of the most powerful and obvious conclusions you can draw from this talk about the uncertain end of your time is that *you can't make plans based on when it's going to run out.*

You can only do what you can with what you have in front of you *right now.*

What would you be doing right now if you knew for a fact that your life would be over in ten years? Five years? One year? Six months?

The trick is to live consciously right now rather than constantly mired in the past or aimless daydreaming about the future. It means focusing on the current state of your relationships, work, health, and finances. It means bringing the most to your miraculous life as you can, and hopefully making a positive impact on the lives of others.

Life passes quickly. It's up to you to harness it, get what you need from it, and give what you owe to it.

Time management, in its essence, is about honoring the spiritual in the Self and finding the true expression of that Self.

There's little more that's spiritual than using your time the best way possible.

Unfortunately, the spiritual part is frequently lost as you blame lack of time, other people, and circumstances for your own failure to manage yourself. You bury yourself in fear, pushing away the spiritual and wasting time chasing things that don't matter.

Remembering this helps deal with the discipline part of time management. You always have the choice to either go after what you want or suffer the pain of hindsight, bludgeoning yourself with "should haves," "would haves," and "if onlys."

And, yes, it can be intimidating and difficult at times. Time management — self-management — is simple to understand, but not easy to do. You must decide and you must act.

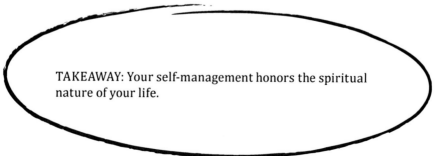

TAKEAWAY: Your self-management honors the spiritual nature of your life.

Lesson 3

Awareness: Waking Up to Your Self

*What is necessary to change a person is to change
his awareness of himself.*

~ Abraham Maslow

*An awareness of one's mortality can lead you to
wake up and live an authentic, meaningful life.*

~ Bernie Siegel

How often do you get to the end of a day and wonder, "Where did my time go? I didn't get anything done today!"

It happens to all of us at some point, but do you find it happening too often?

It doesn't matter how big or small your intentions are — to get a university degree or clean the garage — time just sails by and you're frequently left with little to show for it.

You must find a way to slow the relentless locomotive of passing time.

There is a way, but it can be very challenging. In fact, you might find it to be the hardest part of time management. But, it's also the most important.

You must increase your self-awareness.

Motivational, inspirational, spiritual, religious, self-help, leadership, and psychology books will tell you that very same thing. *The beginning of every road to what you want lies within you.*

You may have spent a lot of time trying to take shortcuts, avoiding or ignoring the messages you've been getting from your Self, and looking for a quick fix or an easy way out.

You may be stuck in the past, holding everyone but yourself responsible for how your life has turned out.

To start priming your mind about awareness, it helps to ask some important questions:

- Do I know where I'm headed?
- Have I determined the most important things that have to get done?
- What am I doing each day to move toward my goals?
- Do I know the best hours of the day to work in order to be most productive?
- How can I get more done than I ever thought possible?

In order to get more done than you ever thought possible, here are some challenging questions you can ask yourself:

- Is it possible that fear is really the thing stopping me from moving forward?
- What am I afraid of?
- Am I getting the results I want? How does my fear affect my productivity and performance?
- Am I wasting time avoiding important issues in my home and work relationships because I'm afraid?
- Are my addictions to television, gossip, blame, excuses, and other things — which waste a lot of time — really about my fear of looking inward and being honest with myself?

The most potent — and scariest — part of self-management is increasing your self-awareness and understanding your fears. When you start to grapple with that, and define for yourself what you *really* want, how you manage your time will change.

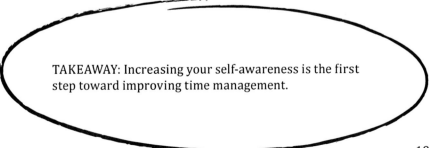

TAKEAWAY: Increasing your self-awareness is the first step toward improving time management.

Lesson 4

Three Cornerstone Questions for Self-Awareness

Know thyself.

~ Oracle at Delphi

To find the courage within you,
give up the quest to become fearless.
Concentrate instead on being fear-conscious.

~ Sarah Quigley and Marilyn Shroyer

You can take all of the questions you asked yourself in the preceding lesson and boil them down to three key questions. If you can answer these questions, you will understand all of the major issues surrounding time management. You will gain clarity about the task before you and you'll find it easier to say no to requests for your time at those times when you should say no.

The three questions are:

1. Who am I?
2. What do I want?
3. How am I going to get it?

These are seemingly simple questions on their surface, especially number two and three, but don't be fooled. These are cornerstone questions that, when answered as fully as possible, will take you on an incredible journey.

They will take you deep inside your Self.

Who am I?

When you pose this question to yourself, you are reflecting largely on your past. Where did you come from? How did your childhood influence who you are today? What habits, attitudes, values, and beliefs did you inherit from those around you? What assumptions and expectations did you *choose to carry with you as truth* that formed the way you look at yourself? How have these impacted your decisions in life? How do they influence how you spend your time?

What do I want?

This question puts you squarely in the present. It will require some imagination about the future, but you have to answer it now, before moving on. In the cold light of day, without considering obstacles, without fear of fear, ask yourself, "What do I want?" The key is to be as specific and detailed (and bold!) as possible and address the major parts of your life: relationships, health, career, finances, and others. The answers you give will be influenced by who you think you are.

How am I going to get it?

This question is about working today to create your future. This is the stage at which you will strategize, plan, and get to work. You'll come up against obstacles and fears, and you will have a plan for dealing with them. You will get frustrated. This is when you will need to remember who you are and what you want. This is where you'll show yourself how badly you want it.

These questions require you to face the brutal facts about who you are, where you are, and how you got there. They will help you define what you want to stop doing, what you will continue doing, and what you will start doing. They may require some forgiveness of yourself and others as well as letting go of long-held beliefs that have kept you stuck.

These are not simple questions with easy answers, but it should be clear that they are directly connected to your time management. If you don't begin to answer these questions, how will you know what to spend your time on?

TAKEAWAY: Answer the three core questions to begin to clarify how you will best use your time.

The Fear List:
What Really Scares You?

How did it get so late so soon?

~ Dr. Seuss

*The greatest mistake a man can make is to be afraid
of making one.*

~ Elbert Hubbard

Ask others what they are afraid of and frequently the initial responses include spiders, snakes, heights, and the dentist.

Probe a little deeper, and the list of fears becomes more delicate, more sensitive, and more profound. Facial expressions change to reveal more intimate secrets. People appear more childlike, as if they are being transported to an earlier moment in time when those fears were initially experienced. At the same time, they look weary from hanging on to those fears for a very long time.

As you ask more people, the list becomes predictable and very familiar. Fear of:

- Making mistakes
- Rejection
- Embarrassment
- Criticism
- Losing approval or love
- Losing control

- Failure
- Success

The problem, of course, isn't the presence of fear. The problem is how you handle fear, what you do with it. There are plenty of successful men and women who feel fear but are not fearful. That is, they are not paralyzed by fear.

In the list above, the focus of power and energy in most of those fears lies with someone else. You give your power away, worrying what others will think of you, letting them judge you and determine your path, instead of living life on your own terms.

Now think about the list of fears in terms of time management. How much time have you wasted trying to be someone you thought other people wanted you to be? Protecting yourself from being vulnerable? Chasing things you thought would bring you happiness only to discover their meaninglessness?

How much time have you wasted worrying what other people thought about you only to realize that they weren't thinking about you at all? How many opportunities passed you by because you were too fearful?

In my 20s, I spent hours and hours in front of the television, worried that anything I did would not be good enough. Therefore, I did nothing. All of that time was wasted because of my fear.

Your time management — your self-management — is directly related to your fears. You put off what you don't like, the things that might cause you to question your abilities, the things that might force you to acknowledge that you aren't everything you thought you were.

It's natural to want to avoid pain; you don't want to feel like you are "less than."

But when you focus primarily on avoiding pain, you frequently waste valuable time that could be spent learning how to cope with the pain and moving forward to get what you want out of life.

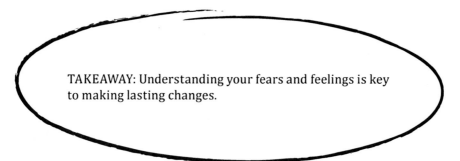

TAKEAWAY: Understanding your fears and feelings is key to making lasting changes.

Lesson 6

Get the Nerve to Handle Fear

We fear something before we hate it; a child who fears noises becomes a man who hates noises.

~ Cyril Connolly

How we relate to fear determines how we do in life, and maybe it is the essence of who we are.

~ Thom Rutledge

What is your fear saying to you?

If you look at the list of fears in the previous lesson, you could summarize it as "I can't handle it."

- I can't handle being embarrassed.
- I can't handle being criticized.
- I can't handle being rejected.
- I can't handle failing.
- I can't handle succeeding.

Your response to this mantra of "I can't handle it" frequently is to make excuses, procrastinate, and give mediocre performances. You fail to be present in your own life.

You're often too busy protecting yourself to realize that time is flying by.

You're often so afraid of the possibility of pain that you treat it as though it's guaranteed and you waste time bracing yourself for the impact instead of doing something about it.

I spent years "protecting myself" from the possibility of criticism and failure. I focused on my shortcomings, my imperfections, and the opinions of others. I convinced myself I couldn't handle most things.

I let massive amounts of time slip by. The sad part is my imagination was full of wonderful things I wanted to do and be.

It doesn't require a sudden, dramatic event in your life to make you believe you can't handle it. It's already happened, slowly, subtly. You created your responses a long time ago, every time you thought you couldn't handle something, every time you thought you weren't good enough. Every time you thought you weren't worthy of Love.

And you play these responses over and over again in your head.

The protective layers built up over the years have pushed in the walls of your comfort zone closer and closer to the point where you don't want to risk very much or take too many chances, if any. In many cases, those walls have also become so thick that breaking through them can be difficult.

Facing fear means starting to understand you can handle much more than you believe you can.

Facing fear means crafting for yourself a new story about your past, one that changes your negative beliefs, assumptions, and thoughts, and, ultimately, your actions.

Facing fear means paying greater attention to what you are doing with your time, having a goal, a system, and discipline.

You deal with fear not by dancing around it or eliminating it, but by going through it — having courage to act not in the absence of fear but in spite of it.

TAKEAWAY: It's time to change your perception and, hence, the reality of what you can handle.

Lesson 7

Excuses and the Blame Game

He that is good for making excuses is seldom good
for anything else.

~ Benjamin Franklin

I don't run away from a challenge because I am
afraid. Instead, I run toward it because the only
way to escape fear is to trample it beneath your feet.

~ Nadia Comaneci

Why is it that some people achieve everything they want and others don't? They all have the same amount of time. And they all have access to the same excuses. What makes them different?

The answer lies in what they choose to focus on.

You can use the blame game as a convenient and comfortable way to disguise fear and to spend time criticizing others. That way, you don't have to face your own shortcomings and take responsibility for the position you're in. Ironically, searching for excuses, blaming everyone but yourself, and being excessively critical of those around you are usually expressions of your own underlying fear.

Unfortunately, this way of being also keeps you from moving forward, from accomplishing what you need to, and from being successful in life.

The blame game can be a way of fostering self-limiting beliefs; excuses are essentially a way for you to quit before you even start.

- But it will be difficult.
- But it will take a long time.

- But there will be family drama.
- But I don't deserve it.
- But I can't afford it.
- But no one will help me.
- But I'm not smart enough.
- But I don't have the time.
- But I don't have the energy.

Attitude distinguishes those who rely on excuses from those who don't. You always have the power to choose your attitude.

You can choose to blame your parents for your lack of progress. You can choose to blame your lack of resources. You can choose to blame an illness or handicap.

Or you can choose to be happy. You can choose to adopt a positive attitude. You can choose to search for the resources. You can choose to fight for the life you want.

Take a minute to consider your blaming practices.

Do you frequently waste time pointing the finger of blame at others? Are you getting what you want out of life?

Have you considered how the two might be related?

Successful people don't look for excuses. They don't blame others for their own failures. They understand that blaming everyone else for their own situations is a trap: It wouldn't get them closer to their goals and it would fill their hearts with negativity and defeat.

TAKEAWAY: Get off your 'buts' and take charge of your destiny.

Lesson 8

Perfectionism:
Striving for the Impossible

Striving for excellence motivates you;
striving for perfection is demoralizing.

~ Harriet Braiker

Ring the bells that still can ring
Forget your perfect offering.
There is a crack in everything.
That's how the light gets in.

~ Leonard Cohen

For many of us, perfectionism plays a major role in our lives. As a recovering perfectionist, I know it influenced the vast majority of my thoughts and actions for years.

My "emotional logic" was: if only I could be perfect, I would be good enough, I would measure up, and I would be acceptable to the people who mattered most.

I operated under a lot of faulty beliefs.

I believed being perfect was a single occurrence, that there was an end point; once I was perfect, everything would be OK. But I learned that the quest for perfection is never finished, even if others do recognize my achievements. It is a constant campaign for validation.

I believed making mistakes and experiencing failure were signs of weakness and an indictment of me as a person. In fact, they are the core ingredients of excellence.

I believed there was one right way, and that right way was the one held by the people I was trying to impress. If they disagreed with my approach, and they were smarter, more experienced, or wealthier than me, then they must be right and I was wrong. In other words, I was not perfect.

I believed other people had their act together. I didn't understand that they might have been fighting their own battles with perfectionism. I didn't understand that they were probably struggling for their own validation. My overriding belief was that everyone was better than me.

I believed everyone had to agree with me and everyone had to like me. In order for that to happen, I had to be perfect in everyone's eyes. In the throes of perfectionism, it's difficult to see the irrationality of this belief.

I believed that through perfect accomplishments I could make myself worthy of Love.

The sin of perfectionism is that it frequently results in procrastination. The sin of perfectionism is that you discount your efforts, your achievements — your life — because of your failure to reach a standard that's actually impossible to meet.

It's important to keep one simple fact in mind: Perfection is unattainable.

What may resonate with you may not resonate with others. Someone will disagree with your point of view or dislike your performance. And that's natural.

I have come to realize that *mistakes and failure — and getting up again — are the keys to success.*

Excellence is different than perfectionism. It's about knowing what you're truly capable of before you begin an undertaking and then doing everything in your power to reach it. It's about striving to be the best you can and not settling for mediocre. It's real and attainable, unlike perfection.

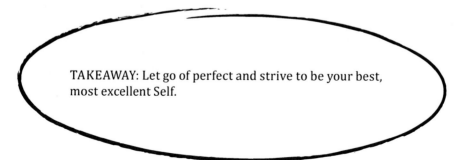

TAKEAWAY: Let go of perfect and strive to be your best, most excellent Self.

Procrastination: Stop Killing Time

*Almost all worry evolves from the conflict between
intuition and inaction.*

~ Gavin De Becker

*Among the aimless you often hear talk about killing
time. People who are constantly killing time are
really killing their own chances in life.
Those who are destined to become successful are
those who make time and use it wisely.*

~ Arthur Brisbane

Procrastination is one of the methods you use in psychological warfare with your Self when you're trapped in a battle with perfectionism.

For me, procrastination was a means of survival, or at least that's how it played in my mind.

When I was growing up, my father was the most influential authority figure in my life. He was bright, educated, charming, and savvy to the ways of the world. He worked hard and was an amazing provider for our family of fourteen.

Along with that came a philosophy that praise was not necessary for a child who was doing what was expected. Only when some extraordinary achievement was reached would there be acknowledgment, and that turned out to be a thumbs-up from across the room.

Over the years, I came to realize that many of his fellow immigrants and others of his generation had a similar philosophy. I'm sure part of it was a profound need to see their children survive in a tough world. After all, that generation had suffered incredible hardships and it needed to keep up the pressure on us to succeed.

Perhaps all would have been lost for me had I not caught my father bragging about his kids to outsiders. He was proud, but it seems he chose not to let that secret known to us in order to protect us from resting on our laurels.

Without my father's acknowledgement and praise, the message I interpreted was that nothing I did would ever be good enough.

But here's the point: He never actually said, "You're not good enough." It was my interpretation of his messages that pushed me into procrastination.

For me, procrastination became a savior of sorts, I believed. On the one hand, when I made a mistake, I felt punished. On the other hand, an excellent performance carried no upside, no praise. I became scared of how hard something would be, so I didn't dive into it. I was afraid of failing at it, so I put it off.

Putting things off meant I could justify my performance with lies to myself like, "I did what I could." "If I only had more time…." "Well, it would have been better if…." You know the drill.

But procrastination isn't that simple. I wasn't just protecting myself. I was still hungry for approval. I still believed that my self-worth was tied to my performance. I ended up paralyzed instead of taking action. I was stuck in the fear of "what if?" What if I'm not good enough? What if people don't like my work? What if it's not perfect?

In reality, my procrastination didn't lessen the belief that I wasn't good enough; it served to *reinforce* that belief — and this had nothing to do with my father.

I convinced myself that I couldn't and so I didn't. I wasn't allowing myself to become my Self.

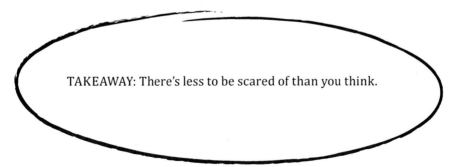

TAKEAWAY: There's less to be scared of than you think.

Lesson 10

Others Care Far Less
Than You Think

*Enjoy your own life without comparing it
with that of another.*

~ Marquis de Condorcet

*Care about what other people think and you will
always be their prisoner.*

~ Lao Tzu

If you are a perfectionist and procrastinator, you likely spend countless hours worrying what others are thinking about you. In essence, you give your power and energy away. You make your life about their opinions, assessments, criticisms, and judgments of you.

Of course, you want to be acceptable and accepted. You don't want to be alone.

But, there are three basic points you should keep in mind:

First, remember the words of Ricky Nelson's song, "Garden Party": "You can't please everybody so you got to please yourself." The simple arithmetic of it is you can't please *everyone*. And you don't necessarily even need to please everyone in your circle. When you strip it down, the number of people you *have to please* is very small.

What you do need are healthy relationships based on mutual respect, concern, consideration, and support.

Second, when you're in the throes of your fear, whether expressed as perfectionism, procrastination, or any other number of ways, you easily forget that those people you're trying to impress have fears of their own. They may even be trying to get acceptance from you and you don't know it.

You spend so much time posing and posturing, worrying and agonizing, in order to get acceptance from others. It's time you tried that hard to get acceptance from yourself.

Third, others simply care far less about what's going on in your life than you think. They think about you far less than you think they do.

I spent countless hours worrying about what people thought of me, trying to manipulate situations to create a favorable response to make me feel good.

I hung on to things they said that struck a nerve — that hurt my feelings — for *years*, agonizing over them and letting them define me. Of course, the people who said those things forgot all about them two minutes after it happened, if they even ever realized it happened.

It's not that they were nasty, mean, or callous. They had other things on their minds than me — like themselves.

Nothing you do will ever be as important to them as their own issues, concerns, and lives.

Nothing you do will ever be as important to them as it is to you.

Now, think about the vast amounts of time you waste — killing your own chances in life — trying to please people who don't really care about how your life turns out. You are sitting in front of the television or computer hoping the fear-inducing task in the other room goes away, and complaining about situations you have absolutely no control over.

It's time to move forward.

TAKEAWAY: Running your life based on what you think other people want is a trap.

Finding the Courage to Move Forward

The best way out is always through.

~ Helen Keller

Love is what we were born with.
Fear is what we learned here.

~ Marianne Williamson

In your mind's eye, you can sometimes look at the big picture, the totality of what you're trying to accomplish, and bury yourself in fear.

So often, you allow the fear to dictate how you proceed. You later find your initial responses to fear unwarranted; you get past the fear and address the task at hand. When you push fear to the side, you frequently find the task is accomplished more quickly than anticipated.

As always, you have a choice. You can allow fear to prevent you from doing things you dream about, or you can find a way to manage your fear and move forward into things you never dreamed possible.

When you realize that everyone — even the most successful among us — has fear, you'll find it easier to move forward.

When you realize perfectionism — not to be confused with excellence — has no role in the creative process, you'll find it easier to move forward.

When you realize the universe is rooting for your success, you'll find it easier to move forward.

When you realize all creativity — life itself — is about taking small steps on a daily basis, here and now, in this minute, you'll find it easier to move forward.

It is useful to reframe how you think about fear. It doesn't take advanced degrees or special talent. Awareness in your daily life will help dramatically reduce the impact of fear and increase your productivity, your confidence, and your satisfaction.

Here are useful ways to reframe your thoughts about fear that will also be part of your time management strategy:

- Understand the difference between healthy fear and paralyzing fear.

- Realize fear can be a result of interpretations of events from childhood, a time when you weren't very good at accurately interpreting what was actually happening around you.

- Resist the urge to compare how you feel on the inside to how others look on the outside. It may appear others are fearless. They're not.

- Develop the habit of preparing well for whatever you set out to do. Proper preparation prevents poor performance, saves massive amounts of time, and goes a long way to reduce fear.

- Don't try to complicate or overthink your task. Just the opposite — KISS: Keep It Super Simple.

- Understand that perfectionism and procrastination are time wasters that keep you from living *your* life.

- Do your best to serve others. When you serve, you can enhance your appreciation for what you have and develop empathy for others. You can put your fear in perspective when you get out of your own head and engage with others.

TAKEAWAY: Moving forward requires courage, not the absence of fear.

Lesson 12

Beating the Fear: John's Story

*They always say time changes things, but you
actually have to change them yourself.*

~ Andy Warhol

*Yesterday is gone. Tomorrow has not yet come. We
have only today. Let us begin.*

~ Mother Teresa

I love telling John's story.

I first met John in January 2013 when he attended my Emotional Intelligence class. "I really need this class," he said. "It's coming at the right time in my life." He was pale, obese, and exhausted.

Two months later, John attended my Time Management class. During one of the breaks he told me his story. "I'm that guy who does only eighty percent of a job around the house. My wife is always pissed at me. And I always wanted to be a stock broker but I never studied for the exam because I listened to the pessimism and negativity of people around me."

He told me that at one point he had "dug up the bushes around our house to plant new ones and never finished it. After your class in January, I went home and finished it. I come outside and find my wife sitting there. I asked her, 'What are you doing?' She said, 'I'm just sitting here admiring the beautiful work you've done.'"

"Since January, I've lost 30 lbs. and I've decided that I will lose another 100. In February, I took my wife and kids to the beach in Galveston. Who goes to the beach in the winter?! We did! And it was great! I'd never done that with my family before. And what's more, I started studying for my broker's exam."

A month later I received another email from John. He'd lost 44 lbs. and was still studying. By June, he had lost a total of 50 lbs. and had revised his weight-loss goal from 100 lbs. to 150 lbs.

One weekend, he was working outside around the house, planting bushes and flowers his wife wanted. She came out and asked, "What are you doing?" John replied, "I'm making those changes you asked for." She got all choked up and said, "You listened to me."

John realized he was the only one 100% responsible for his choices. He realized that his fear, based on his assumptions and his beliefs, had been holding him back. He made up his mind to be different — and changed his life.

John realized he spent more time giving in to his fear than he did living consciously, step by step, day by day. Once he made the shift, he was able to use his time far more productively than ever before.

At the time of this writing, John has lost more than 100 lbs. He continues to study for his broker's exam and has turned his vast knowledge of investing into a new project: writing a book about investing for people who are afraid of investing.

John continues to actively make time for his wife and kids.

Time management is self-management: identifying goals, putting a system in place to get them, and developing the discipline to do it.

John never thought he could have what he has now.

How about you? What do you want to do with your time? What do you want to get out of life? What would you do if fear didn't stop you?

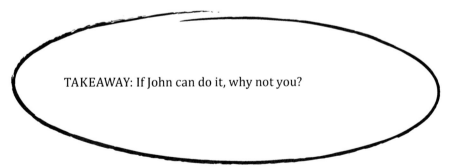

TAKEAWAY: If John can do it, why not you?

Part 2

Goals

Belief: The Foundation of Reaching Your Goals

All that we are is the result of what we have thought.

~ Buddha

It's not who you are that holds you back, it's who you think you're not.

~ Anonymous

Setting goals is one of the most critical parts of time management and self-management. That's what this section of the book is all about.

But many people skip one of the most important parts of goal setting: believing that reaching the goal is possible *before* it becomes reality.

Remember when you used to make New Year's resolutions? Perhaps you stuck with them for a few days, weeks, or even months. But a year was just too long. The novelty wore off and you ran out of enthusiasm.

And yet, year after year, you made the resolutions. And year after year you got the same results. You didn't do a fraction of the things you told yourself you would.

Maybe you didn't really believe it was possible. Lacking the belief that something is possible means it is not possible.

The belief that you can do it helps you clearly define the goal and create a system for getting it. And having a clearly defined goal and system then reinforces your belief in the project, especially when the going gets difficult.

You can go through the motions as much as you want. You can talk about time management, goals, and systems. You can buy countless motivational books. But if you don't believe it, how do you expect to actually get it?

Think about the goals you set for yourself that you didn't reach. Now think about the underlying belief you had around those goals. It might have looked something like this:

> **Goal**: I'm going to lose weight.
>
> **Belief**: I can't lose weight. I've never succeeded at anything.
>
> **Belief**: I've tried before and it never worked.
>
> **Belief**: I don't deserve to be healthy and happy because people always told me I'm no good.

> **Goal**: I'm going to be financially secure.
>
> **Belief**: My parents told me money is the root of all evil, so it's bad to have it.
>
> **Belief**: I don't know how to make a lot of money, so I can't have it.
>
> **Belief**: I can't imagine myself with a lot of money. That would mean I'm successful and I've never been successful at anything.

According to scores of successful people — people who reach their goals and live their dreams — the number one most important ingredient in reaching success is perseverance. But it's difficult to face the tough times if you don't believe in what you're doing or its possibility for success.

How many times have you given up on something when it got difficult? How many times have you given up on something because you just didn't believe you could do it?

Decide what you believe. Without judgment, conclusions, worrying about the road ahead, worrying about what other people will say, worrying about "failing," just pick a goal to go after. Make it small at first. The rest of the book will show you how to get it.

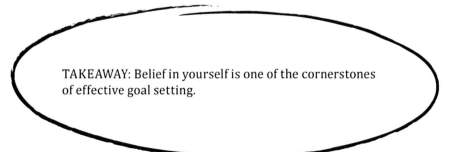

TAKEAWAY: Belief in yourself is one of the cornerstones of effective goal setting.

Priorities:
Knowing What's Important

Action expresses priorities.

~ Mahatma Gandhi

It is not enough to be busy, so are the ants. The question is, 'What are we busy about?'

~ Henry David Thoreau

What's important to you?

If you fail to determine what you believe, it will be difficult, if not impossible, to decide what your priorities are and then set goals that reflect those beliefs and priorities.

It's through the process of establishing priorities that you will also be determining what is *not* worth pursuing. As we'll discuss later, knowing what to say no to is one of the major time management problems many people have. Having priorities helps solve that problem.

In addition, when you determine what's truly important to you, it becomes possible to decide what you're going to sacrifice in order to get it. If you don't know your priorities, you may sacrifice the wrong thing.

One thing should be clear: you will always have priorities.

The question is will they be priorities that you consciously choose or will they just be things that happen to you while you're locked down in fear or just not paying attention?

So often you declare your priorities and yet your actions don't reflect your words. And, by the way, there's really no need to declare your priorities to the world; you will show the world your priorities by what you do.

For example, if you say you're going to exercise and lose weight, but instead you spend hours in front of the television and you eat three pizzas a week, watching television and eating pizza are, in reality, your priorities.

As with belief, establishing your priorities is not an exercise in a vacuum to be done for its own sake. It's a necessary part of moving forward to get what you want. It's part of the foundation for achieving goals and saving time from spinning your wheels.

There are a couple of reasons you must make priorities. First, goals in and of themselves are fine, but if you're chasing the wrong goals or too many goals, you won't end up where you want to go. Second, going after worthwhile goals is frequently a difficult undertaking. If it were simple, everyone would be doing it. If you don't make the right goals a priority, you won't do them. And third, there are always competing activities, interruptions, and distractions that threaten to take time away from your priorities. You have to protect the time you create to pursue your priorities. If you don't know your priorities, it's more difficult to protect your time.

Successful people get what they want because they're very good at understanding those three things.

For me, losing weight was always difficult. When I finally set it as a priority, I understood what needed to be done, how it needed to be done, when it needed to be done, and I did it. I carved out the time to exercise and changed my eating habits. I lost 17 lbs. in six weeks with little stress or anxiety.

Once losing weight became a priority — together with belief — it was a relatively easy goal to reach.

Your priorities are the engine that will influence the choices you make and drive your actions.

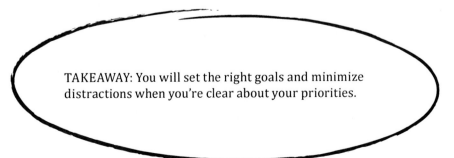

TAKEAWAY: You will set the right goals and minimize distractions when you're clear about your priorities.

Visualization: Seeing Your Future

*Dare to visualize a world in which your most
treasured dreams have become true.*

~ Ralph Marston

*If you want to reach a goal, you must 'see the
reaching' in your own mind
before you actually arrive at your goal.*

~ Zig Ziglar

Once you believe in something and have your priorities, it becomes much easier to move forward. The next step in your plan is to visualize reaching your goal.

It took me a long time to trust this process. When people told me I should visualize where I wanted to go, it sounded like New Age, warm and fuzzy, hocus pocus. "If you can see it, you can be it."

Over time, I came to realize that without visualization, the road would be much more difficult.

Visualizing isn't simply about picturing something; it's picturing yourself in great detail doing that thing. Your brain doesn't know the difference between the imagined accomplishment and the real one. When you step up to do it in "real life," you have already practiced it in your mind, and that makes a difference.

The golf great, Jack Nicklaus, said that before he ever took a swing, whether in practice or in a match, he always visualized the ball "sitting high and pretty and white up on the green."

Arnold Schwarzenegger said while training for the Mr. Universe competition, "I pictured myself on the top spot on the podium, winning first place."

A few years ago I thought it would be great to play in a band on the famed 6th Street in Austin, known as the Live Music Capital of the World. But my brain couldn't visualize it for two simple reasons:

First, I didn't believe I could do it. The old voice in my head kicked in, saying, "Those are great musicians. You can't play with them. You're not good enough." I had little belief.

Second, I had never been to 6th Street, or even to Austin for that matter. Now, you don't necessarily have to physically go to the place where your goal will happen; often it's not possible. But I lived close to Austin and I hadn't even been there.

My first step in helping me visualize my own performance on 6th Street was to go there and see the bands that were playing.

Having a picture in my mind of what 6th Street looked like, I could more easily visualize myself playing there. This cemented the belief and I knew right then that I would do it someday.

A year and a half later, I moved to Austin and a month after that I had my first experience playing at a club on 6th Street.

Visualization is an important part of anything you seek: wonderful relationships, financial success, great job or career, strong family life, or whatever your goal.

Most people won't take the time to try to visualize their success. They don't know what they really want, they don't think it's possible, they can't imagine themselves having something they've never had, and so they don't do anything about it.

They spend their time *talking* about having a life instead of *having* a life.

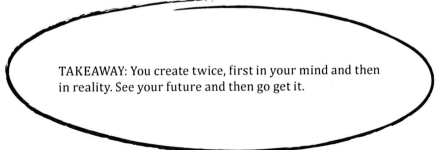

TAKEAWAY: You create twice, first in your mind and then in reality. See your future and then go get it.

It's All about the Choices You Make

You always have two choices: your commitment versus your fear.

~ Sammy Davis, Jr.

Desires dictate our priorities, priorities shape our choices, and choices determine our actions.

~ Dallin H. Oaks

Managing your time — managing yourself — and reaching your goals is all about the choices you make.

There's no two ways about it. This is the Holy Grail of time management. If you don't make good choices, the outcomes you get will reflect that.

If you're wondering where your time goes, look at the choices you make.

If you're wondering why you don't get half the things done you'd like to, look at the choices you make.

If you're wondering why you don't have the success you want — whether financial, health, relationships, career — look at the choices you make.

This is not rocket science. There is no big secret to reaching goals. Your failure or ability to reach your goals lies in the choices you make.

The idea of your own personal choices as the core of your time management is frequently obscured by the games you play to deny your own personal responsibility.

You blame other people for taking your time. *You chose to give it to them.*

You waste time gossiping about others because they don't meet your standards. *You chose to waste that time.*

You complain about how much time it takes to maintain your home. *You chose to buy it.*

It's critical that you start to look at your own life as the result of the choices you make. Every choice ultimately will have an impact on your time and your ability to get the right things done.

Who am I? What do I want? How am I going to get it?

Perhaps one of the most important choices you'll make is that you're not going to let anyone get in the way of you reaching your goals. (And that does not make you a bad person.)

You know that often your lack of progress in a particular direction has been your inability to focus on a specific choice, a specific road. You have either tried to do too many things at once or you started and stopped, started and stopped.

How many times have you "decided" to do something only to find that, after a couple of days or weeks of excited work, you stopped? You were addicted to the initial excitement but you never learned how to actually pursue a goal.

This is a massive waste of time.

The beauty of all of this — and one of the hardest parts — is that you get to choose. You can stay where you are or move forward. You can pursue goals that are really someone else's or you can be courageous and listen to the voice in your heart and pursue your own goals.

Will you choose to let other people stop you? Will you choose to let your fear dictate the road ahead? Will you choose to waste time stuck in fear or wallowing in self-pity? Will you choose to believe that everything that came before dictates everything that is possible in the future?

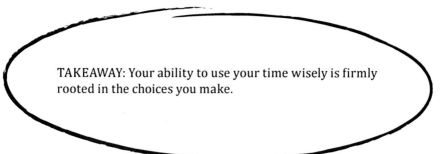

TAKEAWAY: Your ability to use your time wisely is firmly rooted in the choices you make.

Decide, Commit, Succeed

Do or do not. There is no try.

~ Yoda

Until one is committed, there is hesitancy, the chance to draw back. Whatever you can do or dream you can, begin it. Boldness has genius, power, and magic in it. Begin it now.

~ Johann Wolfgang von Goethe

You may dream about things you want, have a desire to live a better life, to have more money, or to improve your relationships. You may have made some good choices.

You may have even clarified exactly what you want and how you're going to get it.

And then you changed your mind. You got bored with what you were doing and distracted by the new shiny object that came into sight.

You set yourself up for failure by skipping one of the most important steps toward reaching your goals: deciding and committing.

When I was in heavy procrastination mode, I watched countless hours of television. I remember the early days of commercials for P90X, the extreme exercise workout regimen, when they could be seen only at two or three o'clock in the morning.

The thing that caught my eye, besides the madness of the workout itself, was the tagline of Beach Body, the parent company of P90X: *Decide. Commit. Succeed*®.

This is one of the easiest reminders to memorize and carry with you at all times. Decide. Commit. Succeed.

Here's a key question to ask yourself: Have I truly decided what I want?

Don't take this word "decided" too lightly. You either decide or you don't decide; there is no in-between. Unfortunately, you may "decide" several times a week: I'm going to do this. No, I'm going to do that. I've changed my mind; I'm going to do something else.

That's not deciding. Either you've decided or you haven't. You can't have it both ways.

Deciding is critically important...but it's not enough. Here's what I mean.

Five frogs are sitting on a log. One decides to jump off. How many frogs remain on the log? The answer, of course, is five. The frog that decided to jump did just that...decided. He didn't actually jump. You can decide all you want, but until you act — with a plan in hand — your decisions don't mean much.

Once you've decided you want to be in charge of your life, that you want to deal with your fear, that you want to go after your priorities, you then ask yourself: "Am I committed to it?" You're either committed or you're not.

Don't fool yourself. You can't be committed to an undertaking and not committed at the same time.

You can't be committed to exercise and health while continuing to eat a lot of junk food. You can't be committed to your marriage and run around on the side. You can't be committed to time management and do nothing to change your self-management.

A commitment is not simply a promise that you're going to do something. It is the action itself. You display your commitment in the doing of a thing. True commitment is staying with the program even when it is inconvenient or difficult.

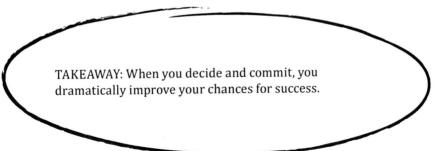

TAKEAWAY: When you decide and commit, you dramatically improve your chances for success.

Lesson 18
Understanding Goals

What keeps me going is goals.

~ Muhammad Ali

You cannot expect to achieve new goals
or move beyond your present circumstances unless
you change.

~ Les Brown

In a very broad sense, you have to decide the aim of your time management: Is it to be productive? Is it to spend more time with your family? Is it to keep your desk clean? Is it to be recognized by the community? Is it to get a promotion and a raise?

Who am I? What do I want? How am I going to get it?

The goals you pursue are part of your self-concept. You pursue certain goals in a certain way because of who you are. In turn, the goals you pursue and the way you pursue them define who you become.

You may be struggling to decide what your goals are. If that's the case, take some time to get clear about what you like in life.

What are your interests, likes, and dislikes? Make a list of your favorite things. Out of that kind of contemplation you will see a pattern emerge of what you like to do and what you don't like to do. Then you can do some research or talk to a mentor or coach about how to proceed.

It helps to establish whether your goal is an end goal or a means goal. Is it a way to simply get to something else or is it ultimately what you're trying to accomplish?

For example, for me, losing weight was a means goal. It wasn't simply to weigh less; it was to be healthier. If I had lost the weight and continued to eat fast food, I would not have reached my end goal of being healthier.

When you state the goal very clearly, it will help you determine the next steps. Just as important, your clear goal will help you determine what *not* to spend time on.

For example, when I started playing harmonica, and later guitar, my goals were the same with both instruments: I wanted to make noise that sounded like music and play well enough to amuse myself. That's it. Quite literally, that was the entirety of my stated goals.

Since I was clear about what I was after, it was easy to choose the right instructional materials and equipment. I wasn't going to spend time learning to read music or studying a lot of music theory because they were not part of my goals. My goals were to make noise and amuse myself.

Being clear with myself also made it easy to tune out people who said to me, "You need to learn to read music." I would just smile and nod. They didn't know my goals and I didn't need to explain them to them.

What is the ultimate result you would like to see come to fruition as a result of your effort, as a result of your time management?

Sometimes the goal you reach may not look exactly as you visualized it. That's normal. In the course of pursuing the goals, conditions may change, your understanding of the process to get the goal may change, or it may be easier or more difficult than expected. These are all normal parts of the process.

The far more important thing is to know whether you have real goals or fake goals. You'll find out in the next lesson.

TAKEAWAY: How you spend your time will be influenced by the clarity of your goals.

Lesson 19

Set SMART Goals

*Setting goals is the first step
in turning the invisible into the visible.*

~ Tony Robbins

*What you get by achieving your goals
is not as important as what you become by
achieving your goals.*

~ Johann Wolfgang von Goethe

Your ability to waste ridiculous amounts of time comes largely from your uncertainty and lack of clarity.

Once you've clarified your beliefs and determined your priorities, it will be easier to identify where you want to go.

After all, if you don't know where you're headed, you'll end up wherever life takes you. You will definitely end up somewhere, but probably not the place you wanted to be.

You need a goal, and a plan to reach that goal.

Whether you realized it or not, that plan started to take shape when you asked yourself the three cornerstone questions: **Who am I? What do I want? How am I going to get it?**

When you do a good job fleshing out the answers to those questions, your path ahead will become clearer. Even if you don't have all of the answers immediately, at a minimum you will already know where you *don't* want to go.

Ultimately, when you do make your goals, it's critical to understand the difference between real goals and fake goals.

Fake goals are vague and ambiguous hopes, desires, and wishes — things that are very difficult to attain. They're resistant to planning; there's nothing concrete about them. "I want to lose weight." "I want to make a lot of money." "I want to have great relationships."

SMART is a simple acronym you can use to remind yourself if your goals are "real" or "fake." SMART goals are the difference between wishful thinking and making real progress.

S — Specific. Your goal has to be as specific as possible. "I want to lose weight" is not a real goal. "I will lose fifteen pounds between January 1st and February 15th and here's how I'm going to do it" is a much more specific goal, making it easier to get started and more difficult to get thrown off course.

M — Measurable. You have to know what it is you are trying to do. How will you know when you've reached the goal? What does "done" look like? In the weight-loss example, done is when the person loses fifteen pounds.

A — Attainable. Is it actually possible to reach this goal? Losing 100 pounds in a week is not attainable, but losing fifteen in six weeks is within reach.

R — Results-oriented. You need to set goals like you set a destination when you get in the car — with the expectation you will get there. The *pursuit* of goals is critical, but you can easily forget that you actually need to arrive at your destination.

T — Time-bound. In the weight-loss example above, the time limit was six weeks. Deadlines are critical when pursuing goals.

When you set SMART goals, you create the context for the goals, the framework that makes them easier to attain.

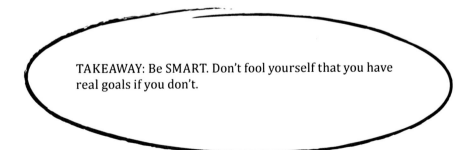

TAKEAWAY: Be SMART. Don't fool yourself that you have real goals if you don't.

Make SMART Goals SMARTER

*Every time I've had a bad performance at an event,
I've come back more determined and focused.*

~ Shaun White

*Courage — the quality of daring to crawl out from
under the covers to respond to fear with fresh
attention and appropriate responses.*

~ Sarah Quigley

The simplest way to make pursuing a SMART goal even more effective is to make it SMARTER.

E — Evaluate. After you've set your goal, build in an evaluation.

Depending on the goal and the plan, evaluation could come at the end of every day if it's a goal that requires daily progress. It could be weekly, monthly, or quarterly. You can make that decision as you set the goal.

The primary function of the evaluation, of course, is to see if the project is going according to plan, if everything has been done correctly, if the project is still on target for an on-time completion, and if anything needs to be fixed or improved.

Whether pursuing a goal at work or home, conditions, support, availability of resources, financing, and a host of other factors may have changed since you set out on your goal. A timely evaluation will tell you if you need to change tactics within the pursuit of your goal in order to stay on track.

R — Re-do. Sometimes this can be the hardest part. After you've gone down the road toward the goal and have done the evaluation, you may realize that parts of the project need to be re-done. It can be difficult to find the energy and patience, especially if it had been a hard slog to get to the point you're at.

This is probably a good time in the process to take a break, if you have that luxury. It could be a few hours or a day or two to recharge your batteries and get into the right frame of mind. In many cases, it will require devising a plan to handle the re-do portion of your project.

It helps to build a cushion of time into your original plan so that when the re-do phase arrives — and it does quite often in projects — you have the flexibility to adjust and adapt without fear.

The re-do phase frequently gets you better results and increased satisfaction. You may be tempted to skip the evaluation and re-do part because you're exhausted, frustrated, or perhaps even lazy.

But realize that this can be the "make or break" time of the entire goal and is worth the extra energy.

For example, when John, profiled in Lesson 12, was in the process of losing weight, his evaluation told him he needed to re-do his goal statement. His progress wasn't as fast as he anticipated.

In the past, he would have simply quit trying, but now that he had a plan in place, he reconsidered his approach and made the necessary changes.

The bottom line is this: What will you do if you fall off the wagon?

Developing SMARTER goals helps reduce fear, minimize wasted time, and get you to your goal faster than you would otherwise.

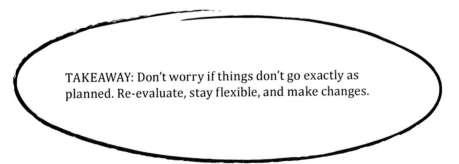

TAKEAWAY: Don't worry if things don't go exactly as planned. Re-evaluate, stay flexible, and make changes.

Lesson 21

Great Questions to Help You Reach Your Goals

You are never too old to set another goal or to dream a new dream.

~ C. S. Lewis

The difference between who you are and who you want to be is what you do.

~ Bill Phillips

Write down one goal you're going to achieve.

As always, you can assess the quality of your stated goal with a series of questions you can ask yourself:

Why do I want to pursue this goal? Is it something I really want to do for myself or am I doing it because others expect it of me? Am I doing it because it will bring me fame and fortune and people will think highly of me?

Am I pursuing this particular goal because I have nothing better to do? Because I don't know what else to do? Because I really don't know what I'm interested in?

Does pursuing this goal get me closer to the overall lifestyle I want to have for myself? Does this goal feed into my overall plan? What other things become possible when I reach this goal?

Is this goal a true priority? Does pursuing this goal take away from other more important goals or priorities I have in life?

Does this goal or priority truly reflect the values I proclaim to have?

Does the goal contribute to the overall mission of the organization, agency, or company where I work? Does this goal help me get a raise or promotion? Am I spending too much time on a petty goal and avoiding more difficult goals? Am I using the petty goal to pretend I'm so busy working when, in fact, I shouldn't be pursuing it at all?

Is my goal Specific? Measurable? Attainable? Results-oriented? Time-bound? If not, how can I improve it? Have I built in an Evaluation stage? Am I prepared to Re-do parts of my work if they aren't up to standard in order to reach the goal?

Now that it's a SMARTER goal, what next steps do I need to take to achieve it?

What tools or resources do I need in order to achieve my goal? Does it require money? Equipment? Work space? Assistance from other people? Who has already done what I'm trying to do? Can I get advice, support, or assistance from those people?

What is a realistic deadline for each step in reaching my goal? When is the optimal time to work on these steps?

Do I have a system in place for reaching the goal over the long-term? Do I have a plan for when pursuit of the goal gets thrown off track? Do I know how I will handle or recover from interruptions, setbacks, or mistakes?

What does "done" look like? How will I know when I've completed my goal?

I recommend writing the answers to the questions above that apply to your situation. When you're finished you will have a great blueprint for getting where you want to go.

TAKEAWAY: With a detailed blueprint in place, it becomes easier to reach your goals.

Prime Time: Not All Hours are Created Equal

*Time is what we want most, but
what we use the worst.*

~ William Penn

*It's really clear that the most precious resource
we all have is time.*

~ Steve Jobs

An important part of effective time management and productivity is to know the best and worst times to do things.

People who accomplish a lot know how to use their prime time, that time of day when they are most rested, most focused, and can get the most work done that will give the greatest return for the time spent.

Here are five questions to help you identify your most productive time:

1. Are you a morning person or a night owl? What time is optimal for you to wake up? When is the best time to go to bed?

2. During what hours of the day are you most alert, awake, and productive?

3. When and under what conditions do you get the most work done? When do you do your best work?

4. When do you do the activities that require most thought?

5. When do you typically get tired? When does your energy start to fade?

Answering these questions for yourself is important since the answers will determine which activities you do at what time of the day.

The number one rule in managing your prime time is to protect it. You don't want to give that time away too easily. Your success will depend in large part on your ability to control that time.

Here are 5 ways to do this:

1. Don't engage in low-value tasks like filing papers, straightening your desk, going for coffee, or returning phone calls of minor importance once your prime time has begun.

2. Minimize distractions as much as possible. Close your office door. Turn off your phone if you can. Let colleagues, staff, or family know you are not to be disturbed. Turn off the TV and the music.

3. Block your prime time on your calendar and call it a meeting. No one has to know that your meeting is with yourself.

4. If interruptions are unavoidable, deal with them quickly and effectively. If you have an administrative assistant, use him or her to help protect your time.

5. Keep on hand a pad of paper or some other means of capturing ideas you may have unrelated to the project you're working on so you can get back to work as quickly as possible.

The nature of your work may be such that you're constantly on the go or always interrupted. You may need to remove yourself from that setting in order to focus on important tasks. Arriving early before coworkers or staying late is also a way to create and protect prime time (but you must use it productively).

At home, your prime time may be early in the morning before anyone wakes up or at night after everyone has gone to bed. Novelist John Grisham wrote his first two novels in the laundry room of his home before everyone else got up. After a few hours of writing, he went to his day job.

You'll know if you're serious about accomplishing your goals by the consistency of your prime time and your willingness and ability to protect it.

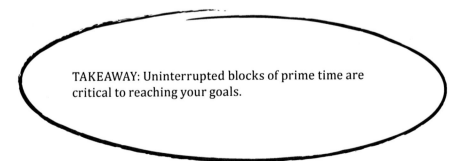

TAKEAWAY: Uninterrupted blocks of prime time are critical to reaching your goals.

Compound Interest and Time

*Compound interest is the most powerful force
in the universe.*

~ Albert Einstein

*Productivity is never an accident.
It is always the result of a commitment to excellence,
intelligent planning, and focused effort.*

~ Paul J. Meyer

When you hear the words "compound interest," your first association is likely to relate to money. One of the roads to wealth is having your money grow at a much faster rate than if there were no compound interest. In short, very rapid progress.

Can you start to think about compound interest in terms of investing in time to pursue your goals?

The common denominator in the case of both money and goals is time: how can you accelerate your progress to reach your goals more quickly?

Let me illustrate this with an example I saw when I worked at a university. I found myself interested in resumes of professors. Why was one professor's resume three pages long and another's was fifteen pages? What was the more productive professor doing that the other was not?

The answer is compounding his time.

The professor with the three-page resume spent a certain amount of time doing research. He wrote several articles and published them in journals. He was proud of his production. Over time, he amassed a series of articles and some lecturing appearances at conferences.

I could see from the second professor's resume that he did more planning and strategizing, organizing and thinking, than the first professor. He spent a certain amount of time doing research but he had determined in advance the things he was interested in and then set out to do his research.

His efforts resulted in many more articles than the first professor. These articles were shaped into a book and published. The same information was used in his university lectures as well as at academic conferences. The information was also used when he gave interviews to the media and delivered training programs at private companies and government agencies.

The second professor was getting far more productivity from his time than the first professor simply by understanding what he wanted to achieve and how he was going to do it. He understood that multiple goals could be met by planning and coordinating his activities.

Instead of each of his activities resulting in one-off products, the second professor had compounded his time to produce much more.

Just as important, the second professor knew how to leverage the resources around him. He mentored students and colleagues in the conduct of their own studies and research; they, in turn, worked with the professor, doing research for him, saving him a huge amount of time.

So, major questions for you to ponder are: How can I compound my time? Are there methods or approaches to my projects either at work or at home that lend themselves to compounding?

What resources do I have access to that can help me reach my goals? Who can help me reach my goals? What projects am I working on that would be of interest to others?

What efforts am I expending that can be used for multiple purposes?

TAKEAWAY: In pursuing goals, think about the possibility of compounding your time.

Turbocharging Your Learning

Productivity is being able to do things that you were never able to do before.

~ Franz Kafka

Each minute is a little thing, and yet, with respect to our personal productivity,
to manage the minute is the secret of success.

~ Joseph B. Wirthlin

I like to refer to compounding time as "turbocharging." You want to get a significant advantage — a big boost — from strategizing about your time and compounding it as much as possible.

Here's an example of turbocharging time that often comes up in my time management workshops.

Many people in my audiences are interested in going back to school, but they resist it because of their fear of the workload. They say to themselves, "I can't handle all of that reading."

I ask them to imagine they're in school and have been given an assignment to read a 250-page book. I then ask them how they will approach the assignment.

Typically, they say things like, "I'll read it from cover to cover," "I'll read it with a hi-lighter." They will read every word of the book from start to finish. But they also know they'll get bored easily and will quickly forget what they read.

Part of the problem is they'll use the same approach to reading today that they learned 25 or 30 years ago. They need a new way of approaching the challenge.

Here's one possibility:

1. Read the title and back cover. They will give you clues about the content of the book.

2. Read the Preface, Foreword, and Introduction. Frequently, broad summaries of the book are presented there. Read the Table of Contents for the whole book. Where is the author taking you?

3. Read the first chapter and the last chapter. This isn't a novel; you won't ruin the book by reading the end first. Then read the first and last couple of paragraphs of each chapter.

4. Now go to the internet to learn about the author if there isn't enough information in the book itself. Is she an academic or practitioner? Is he conservative or liberal?

5. Check booksellers, journals, and other online resources to find out if anyone has written a review, summary, or outline of the book.

6. Check YouTube and other video-driven sites to see if there are any lectures or demonstrations about the topic of the book.

7. Go to Wikipedia and other general reference sites for a background on the subject matter.

If you develop an approach like this, in about an hour you'll have a very good idea of what the book will cover. You'll start reading the book knowing whether it deserves a close read (as for technical material) or if skimming to the important parts is called for.

Another method that turbocharges your learning time is to explore as many books or articles as you can on the same subject at the same time. If you read or skim, say, ten books, you will be exposed to most, if not all, of the fundamental issues and arguments of that topic.

What does this kind of turbocharging do for you?

It can help you get through school, earn a degree, get a better job, earn a higher salary, and be well-positioned for advancement. Possible side effects include greater satisfaction, a boost in confidence, less pressure at home over finances, and the ability to influence more situations and more people.

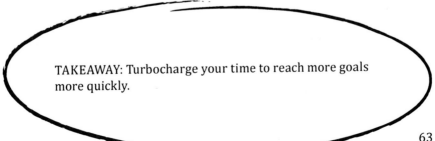

TAKEAWAY: Turbocharge your time to reach more goals more quickly.

Making Time for What's Important: Kandy and Steve's Story

Coming together is a beginning; keeping together is progress; working together is success.

~ Henry Ford

When we can no longer change a situation, we are challenged to change ourselves.

~ Viktor Frankl

Kandy and Steve were like most couples. They were running from chore to chore and errand to errand. They never had time, they told themselves. No time to clean the garage. No time to play with the kids.

Fortunately, they attended my time management workshop together, which meant one wouldn't have to go home and convince the other to make changes. "We both became determined that it was time to change."

In a letter to me, Kandy laid out their plan. "We sat down and made a list of what we wanted to accomplish. We made realistic goals, with achievable dates. As we progress, we mark our calendar and have a 'mini-celebration' when we reach our goal."

Kandy and Steve consciously chose their priorities, set them as goals, and went after them. "We started spending more time outside with our kids. To be able to enjoy their smiles is worth more than anything else."

"We also set up family night, where we either play board games (no technology), talk, sing, or dance. We teach our kids the value of family time and give them a chance to express themselves."

"One of our short-term goals was to tackle the organization of our garage. We determined things that can be used, recycled, donated, and of course my favorite: trash. We accepted the fact that we don't have to keep everything."

"This practice is now being passed down to our kids with their toys. We have a max capacity of two bins for toys and, once that is reached, they have to go through them and determine what they want to keep, donate, recycle, or throw out."

"I believe if we start with them young, it will be much easier as they get older for bigger projects they may encounter with their respective families."

Like John in Lesson 12, Kandy was able to see more clearly her earlier failure to act and was yearning for change. "I was tired of sitting on the sidelines, seeing everyone else succeed and be happy while I moped. I guess I just needed some motivation. So from that day forward, we have been able to make better choices on a personal level as well as professional."

"I realized that although it feels good to help others, when it becomes all about them and you put yourself last, something's wrong. I wrote down the reasons I continued to allow negative people in my life. After making this assessment, I realized the time had come to part ways. Although it was painful at first, I soon felt liberated. No more of the same drama. No more negativity and definitely more time for the things that matter most to me."

Closing out her letter to me, Kandy added this one last piece of sage wisdom: "Remember to make your goals real, write them down. Look at them every day, make a plan, and follow through! Success is only as far off as you make it. Take control of YOUR life!"

It's probably not a coincidence that after making conscious choices, setting her priorities, and organizing her life, Kandy won an award for excellence at work and got a promotion.

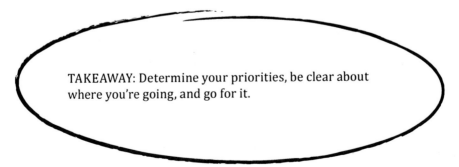

TAKEAWAY: Determine your priorities, be clear about where you're going, and go for it.

Part 3

System

Creating a System

A bad system will beat a good person every time.

~ W. Edwards Deming

Systems are not sexy — but they really do drive everything we do!

~ Carrie Wilkerson

There are two basic ideas about a system that are worth bearing in mind as you go forward.

First, a system will help you get much more done than if you don't have one. Think about some of the biggest systems we have: government and corporate bureaucracies. While many of us think of the word "bureaucracy" negatively, the fact is they are systems that coordinate and accomplish huge projects.

Second, the parts of a system, by definition, are interconnected and influence each other. Changing one part of a system will affect other parts, even if you can't see a direct connection. It's critical to keep that in mind, whether at work or at home.

The various segments of your life, like your finances, relationships, physical well-being, and career, are all connected and make a whole. If you change one, it will impact the others. Turbocharging your time by developing a good system is about positively impacting your highest priorities with the least amount of energy.

For you, your system will not just be about your structure or organization; it will also be about the choices you make. If you say "yes" to this, you will have to say "no" to that. They're interconnected and impact each other.

If you say "yes" to things you don't believe in, aren't your priority, and don't help you reach your goal, by default you will be saying "no" to things you really need and want.

Every time you say yes, it takes away from something else.

The following are basic parts of my system:

- I create routine activities as much as possible. I know it will be easier on my brain if I do the same things at the same times every day whenever possible. This is important because the human brain gets tired easily from making decisions; the fewer decisions I have to make, the more I can get done in the course of the day.

  For example, I know that the first thing I will do every morning is work on the books in the *Get the Nerve* series. I don't have to spend valuable energy wondering what I'm going to work on when I wake up. I go to the gym at lunchtime, then I eat lunch. Dinner is around the same time every evening.

- I know how to handle my food situation. I know that my nutrition, weight, exercise, money, productivity, attitude, mindset, communication style, and relationships are all connected. The more I weigh, the more I tend to snore at night. Excessive sugar wreaks havoc on my body and makes me grumpy.

  I've made certain decisions about food long before the actual moment to decide presents itself. For example, I always say no to dessert at a restaurant. Likewise, I don't keep ice cream or cookies at home, even though I love both. I don't have to challenge my willpower about whether to eat it or not because it's not there.

- I think about my time management when food shopping. For example, I try not to shop when I'm hungry. I'll be tempted to buy junk food if I do. If I buy junk food, it will impact my weight and require me to exercise harder. This will affect my energy level, my mood, and my time.

You get the idea.

TAKEAWAY: Time management is about every aspect of your life. A system will make your journey easier.

Lesson 27
Do a Mind Sweep

*Nothing is so fatiguing as the eternal hanging on of
an uncompleted task.*

~ William James

*People with clear, written goals, accomplish far
more in a shorter period of time
than people without them could ever imagine.*

~ Brian Tracy

There is only one way to effectively track everything you have to do and want to do and that is by clearly knowing what's on your mind and getting it out of your head.

In my programs, I take audiences through a quick mind sweep exercise. Get a piece of paper (or use your computer) and write down everything on your mind. Don't categorize. Don't prioritize. Don't alphabetize. Just write.

As thoughts pop into your head about things that need to be done other than what you're working on at that moment, write them down and then get back to what you were doing.

The point of the exercise is to get out of your mind all of the random, miscellaneous, and worrying things so you can focus on — be present to — the work you need to be doing. In order to be present in my training sessions, audience members do a mind sweep to capture things that don't pertain to the class so they can focus on the topic of discussion.

When you do a mind sweep you'll see what's on your mind, things that are distracting you from paying full attention.

Audience members frequently have 5, 10, 15 things that are bombarding their brains at all times. This is distracting, to say the least. In addition, they will forget at least some of these things, resulting in stress, mistakes, wasted time, and all-too-often having to apologize to someone.

Some people have had the same things on their minds for six months, a year, two years, and even longer. When you've captured everything on paper during your mind sweep, you can see clearly what has been on your mind. If you have projects or tasks you want or need to get done but you can't pay attention to them in the short term, that's fine. You can always come back to them.

You'll know if you have a system that works well because it will capture everything you need to think about, accomplish, or take care of, and your mind sweep page will have very little on it. The point is to capture everything in your system and get it out of your mind.

You don't want to use up valuable brain energy trying to remember to stop at the dry cleaners or take the kids to the doctor.

One day, one of my assistants in my office started laughing loudly. Another assistant asked what was so funny. Since we had shared calendars, everyone could see each other's schedules. My assistant bellowed, "Joe put 'Go to dry cleaner' on his calendar!" She found it amusing that such a seemingly minor thing had gotten space on my calendar.

If it's not off your mind and captured in your system, the odds increase dramatically that you will forget to do it, make a mistake, keep someone waiting, or miss a deadline.

Since everything's connected, when you do a mind sweep regularly, you reduce stress, get more done, and let people down less frequently.

Be aware that, while this may sound easy, it takes practice, mistakes, and more practice in real life. Don't get discouraged. Putting a system in place will change your life.

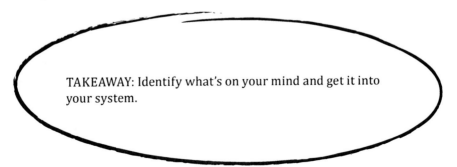

TAKEAWAY: Identify what's on your mind and get it into your system.

Containers: A Key to Success

Out of clutter, find simplicity.

~ Albert Einstein

Order is the shape upon which beauty depends.

~ Pearl S. Buck

Do you ever lose your keys? Do you frequently misplace them? Are you stressed out in the morning even before you leave for work because you can't find your keys?

Ask people who never lose their keys why they don't and they will all tell you the same thing: "I put them in the same place every time."

The idea of well-managed keys illustrates two aspects of good time management. First, it shows that the person has a system. Second, it shows that the person understands how to use containers.

A critical part of an effective system is creating appropriate containers and using them effectively. Containers of one kind or other will make up the majority of your system.

It's easy to think of plastic boxes as containers. Now think about everything else: bookcases, cabinets, closets, hangers, garbage pails, and shelves. These are what I like to think of as space containers. They capture things that take up space.

For example, if you come home from work and put your keys on a hook, the hook is the container. If the keys go in a drawer, think of that as the container. In short, you have a specific place for them that doesn't change.

Now think about your calendar, daily planner, cell phone, notepads, and other tools. I think of these as time containers. They capture appointments, notes, projects, and countless other details in helping you manage your meetings and projects. They capture mostly things requiring time.

Remember the mind sweep: with effective containers, I don't have to try to juggle a lot of information in my mind or try to remember to do certain things. They're captured in my containers. The piece of paper you write your mind sweep on is a container.

When you walk into a Subway sandwich shop, you see a system at work: "Welcome to Subway!" "What kind of bread do you want? You want cheese with that? Do you want it toasted?"

They have a routine; they don't have to think about it.

They have a process supported by containers so they don't have to search for anything while they're building a sandwich. When they're juggling multiple customers, the containers and processes that make up their system help manage their tasks so they don't have to stop to think too much. They just do it.

They are successful because they set themselves up for success.

When you create your system, think about all of the various containers you could use to organize your space and time. Set them up at work and at home. The more specific places you have to put things, the easier it is to manage all of your possessions and responsibilities.

Your life will become easier. You won't have to look for your keys, you won't need to keep stacks of paper all around, there won't be piles of dirty clothes on the floor in your bedroom. You will feel better and work better.

Don't forget to put on your calendar some time every week or two to repair, update, improve, or clean out your containers.

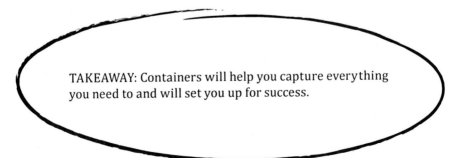

TAKEAWAY: Containers will help you capture everything you need to and will set you up for success.

Get Organized

When in doubt: breathe, drink water, clear clutter.

~ Karen Kramer

I pulled out box after box, setting them haphazardly around the room. My organization lacked something — like, say, organization....

~ Richelle Mead

I used to be a pile person, stacks of paper all over my desk and floor. And I, like many others, convinced myself that I knew where everything was. And maybe I did (more or less).

But how many times did I need to touch the same pieces of paper just to get to the one I was looking for three-quarters of the way down the pile? One thing that helped dramatically was getting organized.

The following steps will help you on your way, whether at work or home:

1. Set aside sufficient time to reorganize. It may be a few hours or even a few days. If it means going in to the office on a Saturday, so be it.

2. Be sure to have new file folders, a label maker, and garbage pail at arm's reach.

3. Find a central location for everything cluttering your place. For example, if you're cleaning your office, gather all of your documents and papers on your desk. Much as in the mind sweep exercise, you are collecting everything that has to be addressed.

4. Establish categories for handling paper. Have a pile for papers to be filed, papers to be acted on, and papers to be read later. Things that can be thrown away immediately go directly into the garbage pail.

5. After all papers have a place in a pile, go through each pile and put each paper in its appropriate place. Do not stop to read them. If it's important enough to keep, create a separate file or scan it into your computer. If not, get rid of it.

6. Get rid of pens that don't work anymore or the 15 pencils that have accumulated.

7. Be sure that everything you need on a daily basis has a place of its own and is within reach of your desk.

As you're going through the organization phase of creating a system and improving your time management, you will need to do the "paper test" for virtually everything you lay your hands on. This test will help you decide what to keep and what to throw away.

- Do I really need it?
- Will it be useful when I need it again?
- Is it new information?
- Is it a necessary part of a project or file?
- Would it be hard to replace?
- Does it have tax or legal implications?
- Will it help me make money?
- Would anything bad happen if I tossed it?
- Would I keep it if I were going to move?

Paper is frequently the bane of your existence, but with current scanning, filing, and storing technologies, it's often easier, more efficient, and more economical to keep documents in your computer or in the cloud.

Reducing clutter also helps reduce stress and frustration, either your own or that of people around you. Have some self-compassion when doing this exercise and celebrate when you're done.

TAKEAWAY: Take the time to get organized now and have the time to do more important things later.

The Right Tools for the Job

Man is a tool-using animal.

Without tools he is nothing, with tools he is all.

~ Thomas Carlyle

We become what we behold.

We shape our tools and then our tools shape us.

~ Marshall McLuhan

One of the big lessons I learned over the years was the importance of having the right tools for the job.

Sometimes you may want to take shortcuts and try to speed up a process that really shouldn't be sped up. Or you don't want to take the time required to really set up your operation before launching it. Fear and overwhelm frequently result when you do that.

The right tools applied to the right mechanism makes work easier, reduces time wasted, and decreases the opportunities for fear to seep inside you. When you have a plan and the right tools, you can set off to work. This is a critical part of your system.

One of the jobs I had at the university when I was studying for the Ph.D. was editor-in-chief of an international magazine that was distributed to twenty-five countries.

Actually, I had volunteered to take on the task. The only problem was I'd never worked at a magazine, let alone run one.

I was scared.

The usual fears arose: What if I fail? What if people criticize me? What if I make mistakes? Of course, I failed a lot, people criticized me, and I made plenty of mistakes.

I started working on the magazine in a very haphazard way. There were stacks of paper all over my desk. With school work on my mind and other projects on my plate, it was impossible to keep track of the material for the magazine.

Eventually, I realized I was trying to do the job without the right tools. I wasn't organized. I was overwhelmed. And I was more than a little stressed out.

The lack of organization and constant stress was costing me time, and lots of it.

The first thing I did was get a system of stacked mailboxes (a container!) and a label maker. I put all the material for each article and section to appear in the magazine in their own boxes, labeling each one. In no time, I had a simple tool to help organize the magazine and the fear diminished greatly. It also happened to be a great time saver.

Next, I created an editorial calendar, with a full production schedule noting all deadlines. Then I spent a few weeks recruiting students (free labor!) from the university to work on the magazine with me. My time spent producing the magazine went from three weeks every month to three days every month while improving the quality.

Sometimes you don't know what the right tools are because you haven't taken the time to fully understand the problem before you or define your goal clearly and specifically enough.

Take stock of your environment, checking to see if you have all of the right tools for the task you're trying to accomplish. You may need to spend a little money. Don't think twice about it. It will be well worth the expense, saving you time and aggravation and dramatically reducing your fear.

TAKEAWAY: The right tools for the job make building your system and maintaining it much easier.

Rethinking Your To-Do List

Sometimes our stop-doing list needs to be bigger than our to-do list.

~ Patti Digh

The only thing more important than your to-do list is your to-be list. The only thing more important than your to-be list is to be.
~ Alan Cohen

With some fundamental pieces of your system taking shape, you're geared up to get to work.

Often, you make yourself a to-do list and almost immediately you're overwhelmed by how much you have to get done. While lists can be critical to accomplishing tasks and reaching your goals, they have to contain the right things.

Follow the 80/20 rule: 80% of your output come from 20% of your inputs. So, if you're in business, around 80% of your revenue should come from 20% of your clients; 80% of your output should be produced by 20% of your time. What few activities can you engage in that produce most of your results?

A to-do list filled with small, minor things will not get you there. When you write a lengthy to-do list, it typically gives all items the same weight. Most often, you'll pick the easiest, most fun tasks so you can get the rush of crossing them off your list.

Unfortunately, these items are usually not the most important ones; the most important get pushed off to another day until you've run out of time and then race to get them done in a panic.

As a result, you perpetuate the myths of your life: "I'm so busy." Yes, but you're busy chasing the wrong things. "I work well under pressure." The self-created pressure due to putting off the most important things until the last minute hurts you more than it helps you.

At the end of your day, you're still frustrated because there are so many things left undone on your to-do list, including the most important.

So let's approach the to-do list a bit differently.

First, stop calling it your to-do list. That sounds like drudgery. Call it your success list. That's the list that contains the items you need to do in order to race toward success.

Second, write a master list. This is a list of all the things you need to get done. When you're done with this list, you'll know everything — small, big, minor, major — that has to get done. This is not to be confused with the mind sweep, which is an exercise to identify what's on your mind, not a list of what has to be done.

Next, take from your master list the three most important things that will give you the greatest push toward your top priorities. Make them as specific as possible. If you put "write book" on your success list, your brain can't really process what that means. It's too big and too scary and you end up doing very little of it.

Fourth, do those three things. They may take two hours; they may take all day. Plus, you're going to be interrupted while you're doing them. If you finish early, go back to the master list and get another high-payoff task to do.

Last, write tomorrow's three-item success list before you finish your workday today. This way you don't waste your prime time tomorrow morning trying to figure out where to start.

See how beliefs, vision, priorities, and goals are coming into play here? Your success list is the reason it's critical to know where you're going, otherwise you'll keep chasing all of the small inconsequential things.

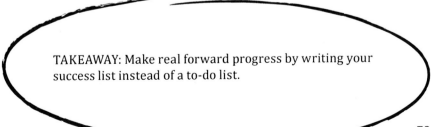

TAKEAWAY: Make real forward progress by writing your success list instead of a to-do list.

Lesson 32

Managing Your Calendar

*The key is not to prioritize what's on your schedule,
but to schedule your priorities.*

~ Stephen Covey

*Plan your progress carefully, hour-by-hour,
day-by-day, month-by-month.
Organized activity and maintained enthusiasm are
the wellsprings of your power.*

~ Paul J. Meyer

It's becoming clearer what should appear on your calendar: things that absolutely have to get done.

There are various ways to manage your calendar, and you'll have to experiment to see what works best for you. Remember, the critical thing is to get everything off your mind and into your system.

I have three calendars. The first is the calendar in my computer. It's synced with my wife's calendar so we know each other's activities and availability. It's also synced to the calendar in my phone.

On that first calendar, I list high-priority work activities like marketing, newsletter and blog writing, speaking engagements, travel, networking meetings, and appointments.

I also schedule errands I have to run. If I'm going to a meeting or a speaking engagement, I'll want to get other things done while I'm out. They have to be on the calendar so I don't forget to do them. I try to keep petty things off my mind and frustration to a minimum.

My second calendar is a Franklin planner. It's laid out in such a way that makes it easy for me to write my master list and my success list in it. I use it primarily to tackle my priorities when I'm working at my desk, track the various elements of projects that have to get done, and make notes to myself.

My third calendar is a monthly wall calendar in my office. It's used to track three high priorities that I do almost every day: book writing, exercising, and playing the guitar.

Each day I work on my manuscripts, I put a black stripe on the calendar; for exercise it's a blue stripe; for playing guitar it's a red stripe. Those three things are important to me. If I don't have a visual way to track them easily, I can fall into a rut of not doing them.

If I get especially busy with work, I can see at a glance the last time I did those activities. At the beginning of every week, I post my goal weight in the box for the following Saturday. All of this makes it easier to remember to do the things I value highly and make my success easier to reach.

These three calendars together capture everything I have to do. And it's not convoluted or confusing because I'm not copying items across calendars and I'm not constantly juggling calendars. They're easy to use and manage.

When you actively use your calendar to capture what has to be accomplished during the day, it helps you say no to requests for your time, which we'll talk about later.

Here are a few more ideas about managing your calendar:

- Schedule routine activities, meetings, errands, and even time for yourself.
- Don't make commitments without consulting your calendar.
- Sync your computer and phone calendars for easy access to both.
- Create shared calendars both at work as appropriate and with your family members.
- Color-code calendar tasks to indicate different people's activities when appropriate.

TAKEAWAY: Your calendar is a key part of your system to track your time and manage activities.

Lesson 33

Handle Your Telephone
So It Doesn't Handle You

I stay away from the telephone if at all possible.

~ Lee Trevino

*My mind is constantly going. For me to completely
relax, I gotta get rid of my cell phone.*

~ Kenny Chesney

The first and most important thing when strategizing about how to handle telephone calls is to understand what I call "the nature of the beast."

What kind of work or family life do you have? What role does the telephone play in it? How much flexibility do you have in managing your incoming and outgoing phone calls?

Once you're clear about this, it's easier to devise a strategy for handling the phone.

If you work in a place that is dependent on the telephone, obviously it will be impossible to simply ignore it or turn it off.

If you work alone from home and the telephone is not a critical part of your business, you can turn it off for a specified amount of time in order to focus on projects.

You may think you fully know your responsibilities and flexibility with your phone at work, but don't make that assumption.

For example, a participant in one of my programs asked how to increase her productivity, particularly since the telephone interrupted her so often. The frequent interruption was breaking her focus. She had to re-read her work and try to get back in the flow of what she had been working on after every call.

I asked a simple question: "Are you required to answer the phone when it rings?" "No." "So why do you answer the phone?" "Because it was ringing," she responded. In that session, she gave herself permission to change her phone habits.

Understand your priorities at home as well. A ringing phone doesn't have to be answered. After a while, your friends and family will know that you never answer the phone during the dinner hour or after 7:00 pm, for example. In most cases, you don't have to be available to everyone all the time, 24/7/365.

Here are ten suggestions you may be able to apply to your situation:

1. Your cell phone has an on/off switch. Use it whenever possible.

2. Screen your calls.

3. Don't return calls during your prime time unless it is a key part of your job.

4. Schedule a time to return calls and bundle them as much as possible.

5. Limit social conversations at work.

6. Do minor tasks that don't require mental effort when on calls that don't require high focus.

7. At the beginning of a conversation, say, "I'm calling about these three things." Cover those three things and get off the phone.

8. To wind down a conversation, signal with, "Before we hang up, let's cover this one last point."

9. Keep the next project you're really interested in on your desk to encourage you to get off the phone.

10. Call people right before lunch and right before closing time when possible. They won't want to stay on the phone with you too long.

These are just a few ways to manage telephone calls and reduce interruptions to your most important work of the day.

TAKEAWAY: Strategize about how to use the phone to get the most out of your day.

Lesson 34
Reducing Email Distractions

*One look at an email can rob you of
15 minutes of focus.*

~ Jacqueline Leo

*Email is familiar. It's comfortable. It's easy to use.
But it might just be the biggest killer of time and
productivity in the office today.*

~ Ryan Holmes

The "nature of the beast" discussed in the previous lesson applies to email as well. What kind of job do you have, what role does email play in it, and how much flexibility do you have in managing your email?

What is it you're using email for and when? Do you answer emails immediately because it gives you a psychological boost or perhaps it soothes some kind of anxiety?

Pay attention to how you feel when you open your email every morning. Does having 2,000 emails in your inbox stress you out at all? Do you take time to clean out your email, send emails to their respective folders, and make sure you haven't missed anything?

The idea behind time management — self-management — is to try to make your life more rewarding, more meaningful, and more fun. Technology is to support your goals, not become the goal.

You can use your calendar to schedule times to email specific people or bundle email reading, writing, and answering for specific times of the day.

When email runs your life, it will interrupt you constantly and keep you from focusing on projects. You must understand the nature of the beast and come to terms with whether you use email as a tool or a crutch. Remember that answering emails does not necessarily make you productive or address your priorities.

The main goal is to ensure that you are not constantly distracted and interrupted by seemingly urgent matters that ultimately are not that important or not important at all. Here are 10 ways to manage your email:

1. Strive to keep your email inbox empty.

2. Answer emails together as much as possible, using non-prime time to do it.

3. Let emails accumulate for a period of time before distracting yourself from your main work to answer them.

4. Follow the two-minute rule: If it can be dealt with in two minutes or less, deal with it.

5. Use flags to keep the most important and urgent emails clearly visible.

6. Turn off notifications, beeps, pop-ups, and any other bells and whistles that distract you from the main task at hand.

7. Divert spam to junk mail as much as possible.

8. Unsubscribe from lists, newsletters, blogs, and services that you are not reading and do not need (except mine).

9. Create sufficiently clear labels so you know where you have stored things.

10. Use the search function when looking for a specific email.

Remember: Pursuing your priorities and reaching your SMART goals is what matters most. Don't be fooled that trying to juggle 10 things at once and non-stop interruptions are a sign of multitasking and increased productivity. In all likelihood, they are just the opposite.

Experiment and develop your own strategy for handling your email.

TAKEAWAY: Be sure to control your email before it controls you.

Use Technology at Home

The real problem is not whether machines think but whether men do.

~ B. F. Skinner

Technology gives us power, but it does not and cannot tell us how to use that power. Thanks to technology, we can instantly communicate across the world, but it still doesn't help us know what to say.

~ Jonathan Sacks

Of course, technology at home is no less important an issue than at work when it comes to time management. You want to make your life as easy as possible while managing your time to do meaningful work and have fun.

With that in mind, as I've mentioned, you want to create a routine around your regularly occurring chores and tasks whenever possible.

Home life is difficult to manage. With kids, a spouse, ex-spouse, relatives, chores, hobbies, and school activities, there are countless things vying for your attention.

But you must be clear about what you're doing, why you're doing it, and how you're getting it done. So often you feel like there's too much to do, but in reality you're doing a lot of things that technology could be doing for you.

I mentioned at the beginning of this section the idea of losing your keys, having to look for them, and the stress it causes even before you leave the house to go to work. The hook you put your keys on is an example of technology. It will work for you and help reduce stress.

"Technology," in its broadest sense, does not have to be electronic or computer-based and it doesn't need to be expensive. They are tools to make it easier to get things done.

Here are some technologies to use around the house to save time and money and reduce frustration and stress:

- Shower cleaner — I was happy when my wife introduced me to Scrubbing Bubbles Automatic Shower Cleaner. Simply hang it in your shower. When you finish a shower, press the button on the dispenser and the cleaner automatically sprays soap in a ring around the shower wall and curtain.

- At-home dry cleaning — Put your clothes in the dryer with a single sheet of Woolite Dry Clean at Home for 20 minutes, take them out, hang them up, and you're good to go. I save time in not having to stop at the dry cleaner as often and I also save a lot of money. If the clothes come out with some light wrinkles, move on to the next item below.

- Clothes steamer — Ironing boards are either a hassle to set up every time I need it or it simply becomes a rack for clothes, mail, and other things. Put your clothes on a hanger, hang them on a hook or the top of a door, and pass the handheld steamer up and down the clothes. It's quick, easy, and beats wrestling with an ironing board.

- Pre-printed shopping list — A lot of people use handwritten shopping lists. A lot of people also forget things when they go shopping. A pre-printed shopping list has all of the major categories and items listed with boxes next to them. Simply check the box of the item you need, tear the sheet off the pad, and go shopping. Without. Forgetting. Anything.

These are just a few simple examples. There are countless ways to introduce technology into your life to make things easier and save you time. Visit places like Office Depot, Home Depot, The Container Store, and others online to see what's available to make your life easier.

The real issue is that so often we just keep using the same set of habits and reflexes we've developed without taking time to consider new ways of doing things.

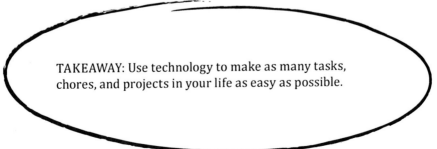

TAKEAWAY: Use technology to make as many tasks, chores, and projects in your life as easy as possible.

Screen Time:
Use It to Your Advantage

Television: A medium. So called because it's neither rare nor well done.

~ Ernie Kovacs

The average family spends 30 hours in front of a television, and they say they don't have the time to have a balanced, integrated life.

~ Stephen Covey

When it comes to time management, your use of screen time is a bit of a double-edged sword. (Think of screen time as television watching, internet browsing, social media use, videogame playing, FaceTime.)

On the one hand, there is truly a tremendous amount of garbage on your screens. It's a massive time suck that distracts and derails you from having the life you truly want. It pulls you in, sedates you, paralyzes you, and makes it easy for you to freely give up your valuable time.

On the other hand, your screens expose you to news, information, knowledge, and entertainment. It tells you about the world around you, helps you relax at the end of a day, and becomes a way to connect with other people through conversation about what you saw on the screen.

Yes, there's plenty of garbage on your screens and there's plenty of good to be said about it.

The real question to ask yourself is this: Is my use of screens an expression of my priorities or is it undermining them?

If you declare that improving your family relationships is a priority, are you fooling yourself that sitting around the television not talking to each other is an expression of your priority?

If you want to improve your health, are you spending your exercise time in front of the screen eating cookies and ice cream?

Perhaps the topic of screen time is where we see the most potent demonstration of time management as self-management.

The time of my life that was most productive, other than now, was when my television antenna was not hooked up to the outside world. I had a VHS player and a DVD player. I watched movies, TV shows, and music instruction through these. I didn't have a computer or internet at home.

During this period, I earned my Ph.D., learned to play guitar, wrote several books, taught at a university, ran an international magazine, had a full-time job, and traveled to several countries, among other things.

Personal growth guru, Brian Tracy, poses a thought-provoking question. He asks, "How much does your television cost you?"

Most people answer the question by saying how much they paid for their television. But Brian comes back to say that television, as a time pit that most of us use for relatively passive entertainment for hours on end every day, costs you $30-40,000 a year.

In the time you spend watching your screens, getting relatively little return for your time investment, you could be learning a new skill, getting a degree, reading, and so on. In other words, you could be pursuing activities that could make you an extra $30-40,000 a year. That's how much your television is really costing you, says Brian.

With multiple ways to watch or record television shows these days, you can build your viewing time around your schedule, making sure you're not using your prime time for mindless television.

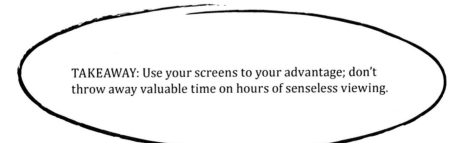

TAKEAWAY: Use your screens to your advantage; don't throw away valuable time on hours of senseless viewing.

Lesson 37
Handling Interruptions

Other people's interruptions of your work are relatively insignificant compared with the countless times you interrupt yourself.

~ Brendan Behan

Many people feel they must multi-task because everybody else is multitasking, but this is partly because they are all interrupting each other so much.

~ Marilyn vos Savant

One of the biggest problems you're dealing with is interruptions. And it's also one of the biggest excuses you're using for not getting things done.

Of course, part of it will be "the nature of the beast," depending on your line of work and your family situation. There are times you just can't avoid being interrupted, especially if it's your supervisor at work or young kids at home.

There are so many more times you allow yourself to be interrupted and then blame it on someone else.

Or, as Irish poet Brendan Behan suggests above, you interrupt yourself countless times each day; most of the time you may not even realize it.

The Unwanted Visitor

You know the person who pops into your office for a 1-minute question and stays for 20 minutes. Or the one who is constantly appearing in your doorway or at your cubicle to chat about American Idol or what their kids ate for dinner last night. It's up to you to deal with that interruption effectively. Here are a few ideas:

1. Simply say you're busy and can't talk or help them at that moment. This is the easiest approach and one that people seem to have difficulty saying.

2. Stand up to talk. If it appears this isn't enough of a hint, head to the coffee machine to refill your cup or to the water cooler and talk with them on the way. Deliver them back to their office, not yours.

3. If you have an office door and work policies don't prohibit closing it, close it. Lock it if necessary.

4. If you need to have a chair in your office but you don't want unwanted visitors getting comfortable, keep a stack of books on it.

Self-Sabotaging Interruptions

If you tracked your interruptions, you very well may find that you are the cause of most of them, even though you may love to complain about other people stealing your time.

1. When you need to deliver a document to someone's office, scan a document at the copier, and so on, put them in the corner on your desk and do it all at once.

2. Social phone calls can quickly get out of control if you let them. Either screen the call or get right to the point of the call.

3. Put in place a system for handling telephone, email, and unwanted visitors so you know in advance how you'll to respond to them.

Home Interruptions

1. You can turn the telephone off at home if you don't need it for family members.

2. Decide who's running your house, you or the kids. Set times when the kids aren't allowed to bother you, especially if you're working on a specific project or hobby.

3. Don't interrupt your kids when they're focusing on something important like homework, otherwise you're treating their work as less important than what you have to say. Developing focus is critical to getting things done.

TAKEAWAY: You can do in 20 uninterrupted minutes what it takes to do in 60 interrupted minutes.

Part 4:

Discipline

Moving Toward Discipline

*Discipline is the bridge between
goals and accomplishment.*

~ Jim Rohn

*I think self-discipline is something, it's like a muscle.
The more you exercise it, the stronger it gets.*

~ Daniel Goldstein

One of the most frequent comments I get is that people don't have the discipline to manage their time, to go after what they want, to maintain the level of intensity needed. They get distracted, run out of steam, and drift away from the task at hand.

Guess what? So do I. So do a lot of people.

The real problem is too many people misunderstand discipline, willpower, and energy. Discipline is not about staying intensely focused at a high level throughout your work day and summoning willpower whenever you need it, at a moment's notice. Willpower is finite and it is exhausted relatively quickly.

They set themselves up to fail because they don't protect their prime time, they don't know how to say no to requests for their time, and they are often chasing the wrong things. They fall back into fear and excuse mode and refuse to face the brutal facts about what's not working in their lives.

They continue doing the same thing over and over expecting a different result.

You may be surprised to know that most of the challenge of discipline is addressed when you clearly define your priorities and goals, and create an effective system to pursue them.

For example, the whole purpose in identifying and effectively using your prime time is to know when your energy, focus, and willpower are strongest so you can get the most important work done. You then do less important, less demanding things when your energy and willpower have decreased.

When you organize yourself, set up containers, write a success list, get the right tools for the job, and manage your technology, a lot of the discipline you thought you lacked is transformed into habits and routine. Having identified your beliefs, visualized the road ahead, and started on your journey, you transform the drudgery of discipline into the excitement of passion.

So, an important part of discipline is to understand yourself and your energy and put in place tools and techniques to take greatest advantage of periods of high focus and concentration.

I rarely do anything from about 1:30 to 3:00 in the afternoon that takes a lot of energy or concentration. That's when my energy is lowest, and I'd be trying to force discipline and willpower.

When I write my success list the night before, I require little or no discipline in getting my day started the next morning.

If I need to lose weight, I don't keep cake, candy, and junk food in the house. Therefore, I don't need to find the discipline to stay away from it.

I don't surround myself with negative people and I don't give away my time easily.

TAKEAWAY: Set yourself up so that your progress doesn't rely solely on discipline and willpower.

Mastering Your Mastery

*If people knew how hard I worked to get my
mastery, it wouldn't seem so wonderful at all.*

~ Michelangelo

*Goals exist in the future and the past.
Practice, the path of mastery,
exists only in the present.*

~ *George Leonard*

Mastery is the path to excellence and should be the daily goal when pursuing the most important priorities of your life.

When you truly understand that mastery itself is a goal, you will find yourself attaching higher value to the things you spend your time on and choosing fewer things to pursue.

Mastery takes time. It takes patience and perseverance, critical ingredients in your success recipe.

Though you may not think of it quite this way, mastery is required if you want to reach a high level of functioning and it includes areas of your life that go beyond the workplace.

Great relationships require mastering your emotions, understanding the needs of other people, choosing your words carefully, and being willing to listen with an empathetic ear.

Great health requires mastering your nutrition, exercising properly, and maintaining fitness.

Great financial health requires mastering your spending, investing in your future, and understanding the value of money.

You get the idea.

You can easily see from the above that the process of mastering is not about perfection; it's about trying, failing, learning, progressing, and trying, failing, learning, and progressing some more.

This is the main reason fear of making mistakes and fear of embarrassment are so important to conquer; they are obstacles standing between you and your success.

Unfortunately, most people don't address these fears and, consequently, live most of their lives in "good enough" mode, protecting themselves from facing fear. Working toward an ideal over time is then replaced by short attention spans and instant gratification that help people pretend they're progressing when they're not.

Short attention spans and instant gratification are among the enemies of great time management. One of the cornerstones of time management is working toward your goals day in and day out over a long period of time.

Just about anyone can be focused for a day or a week or a month, but it's mastering beliefs, priorities, and goals over the long term that is the true core of time management and accomplishment. Decide, commit, succeed.

Mastery is difficult; if it were easy, everyone would be doing it. It's critical to simplify your life as much as possible so that you have the energy and reserves to master the most important things and reap the rewards for doing so with as few distractions as possible.

You need to create routine, tools, techniques, and methods for helping you get what you want so that your energy and brain power can be dedicated to the core of your work: mastering your mastery.

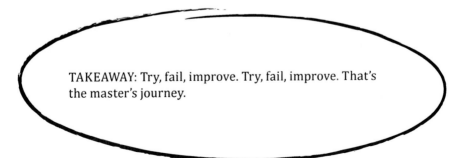

TAKEAWAY: Try, fail, improve. Try, fail, improve. That's the master's journey.

Learn to Love the Plateau

Patience and perseverance have a magical effect before which difficulties disappear and obstacles vanish.

~ John Quincy Adams

Never give up, for that is just the place and time that the tide will turn.

~ Harriet Beecher Stowe

When you try something new, your first steps are frequently filled with mixed emotions. You set out on a steep learning curve and seem to be absorbing so much very quickly. It's exciting and fun.

At the same time, you can feel anxious, uncertain, clumsy, and filled with trepidation. After all, learning something new can be scary. It'll force you to leave your comfort zone.

After a while, though, it will seem you're not making as much progress as you had been. The excitement and novelty of your new venture starts to wear off, and you become frustrated when you hit a plateau.

While it may feel like you have stalled, this is actually a natural occurrence. Most of the time, you won't remain on a steady, upward path; there will be ebbs and flows in your progress.

The plateau — especially the first one — is where you may give in to your frustration and simply quit.

With a mindset of frustration, impatience, and fear, it can be difficult to realize that another leap of progress is waiting up ahead.

The trick is to understand that plateaus happen, and fairly often. You have to be prepared to ignore the voice inside your head when it says, "See, I told you this was going to be impossible."

When successful people reach the plateau, they simply keep going — without judgment, second-guessing, or quitting — and continue to work. They continue to master their mastery.

They know that plateaus are an important part of the process of continuous learning.

Plateaus give your brain time to digest and make sense of what you're working on, preparing you for the next leap of progress.

When I was first learning to play guitar, my fingers were clumsy and I couldn't make the chord changes very easily. I reminded myself to take my time, to expect obstacles, and to remember that if I do the best work I could on a regular basis, I'd see a big jump in progress after some time on the plateau. That's exactly what happened.

It's critical to make the connection between the plateau and time management. Far too many people quit something and start something new, and then when they hit the plateau in the new activity, quit again. Or they stop an activity only to start it up again at a later date.

These are massive wastes of time that are driven primarily by fear and uncertainty. Knowing that plateaus are natural, necessary, and temporary will help you continue on the path you set for yourself and help you use your time more wisely.

TAKEAWAY: Understand that staying on the plateau is a critical part of your process to reach mastery and success.

Multitasking is Worse than a Lie

Multitaskers are just lousy at everything.

~ Clifford Nass

Multitasking is merely the opportunity to screw up more than one thing at a time.

~ Steve Uzzell

There are only two words to say about multitasking: Stop it.

We often hear people claim they are great multitaskers. The problem is researchers know multitasking is impossible.

Multitasking is the *apparent* simultaneous performance of two or more tasks by a computer's central processing unit. The tasks only *appear* to be occurring simultaneously; the same thing happens when you think you're multitasking.

You're really switch tasking, an attempt to perform two or more tasks at the same time *that require mental effort*. While you may think you are doing two things at once, you are really switching back and forth very quickly between tasks.

But you say, "Wait a minute! I can do two things at once!" That's background tasking: when you perform two or more tasks where only one of those tasks requires mental effort.

In *The Myth of Multitasking*, author Dave Crenshaw has a great exercise: On a piece of paper, write the letter 'M' and underneath it write the number 1. After 'M,' write the letter 'U' and then underneath that, the number 2. Alternate between letter and number until you have written the sentence, "Multitasking is worse than a lie" and the numbers 1 to 27. Timing yourself, you'll find that it takes approximately 75 seconds; you'll make mistakes and get confused switching back and forth between letters and numbers.

Now repeat the exercise, only this time write the entire sentence, "Multitasking is worse than a lie," and then underneath write the numbers 1 through 27. This time you will do it in approximately 35 seconds with virtually no mistakes and no confusion.

In the exercise above, think of the line of letters as an activity, like typing an email. The line of numbers is you speaking with someone at your desk. How many mistakes do you think you'll make writing the email when you try to talk to the person at your desk at the same time?

Part of our discipline in managing our time and managing ourselves is to understand that we don't have unlimited supplies of energy. The more complex the task, the more energy it will take to complete. Multitasking dramatically increases the complexity of what your brain is trying to do and sucks up massive amounts of energy.

When trying to multitask, you will actually lose time and energy rather than save it.

Researchers estimate that you lose about 28 percent of an average workday to multitasking ineffectiveness. You'll make mistakes; you'll have to redo work that wasn't done right the first time; and the quality of your work will suffer.

The ultimate result, says Gary Keller, founder of Keller Williams Realty and author of the bestselling book, *The One Thing*, is that "multitaskers experience more life-reducing, happiness-squelching stress."

The funny thing is you certainly didn't set out for life-reducing, happiness-squelching stress when you decided to juggle multiple things. It might be time to reconsider your multitasking practices.

TAKEAWAY: Focusing on one task whenever possible makes for higher-quality work and less stress.

Lesson 42

Break It Down

How do you eat an elephant? One bite at a time.

~ Bill Hogan

Order and simplification are the first steps toward the mastery of a subject.

~ Thomas Mann

One of the best ways to muster the discipline to accomplish something difficult is to break down a complex task into its component parts. Suddenly, it becomes much easier.

All too often, looking at the entirety of a project can be overwhelming and frustrating. You may think that it will be too difficult and decide not to do it, or you'll drag your feet in getting it done.

Breaking it down reduces frustration, makes it easier to stay focused, and easier to stay on the plateau when things don't go as well as you'd like. With smaller pieces to digest, you will see progress more often than trying to attack the whole thing at once. And this progress will help create momentum, cement belief, and instill hope.

It's easier to build routine, attention, focus, and mastery around smaller projects. It also reduces the temptation you may feel to multitask in order to try to get the impossibly large project finished.

In workshops, I often use a guitar to illustrate breaking down complex tasks. I pick up the guitar and ask people how they would feel if I told them they would have to play something on it in a couple of weeks.

If they don't already know how to play, they freak out and already assume it's impossible. That's because they are looking at the task as one big scary whole instead of breaking it down.

Their fear is already getting inside of them and they haven't even begun to understand the possibilities for the road ahead.

In five minutes, I teach them to play the guitar. And, with what I show them, they will be able to play thousands and thousands of songs.

I do this by breaking down the idea of playing the guitar into simple components. I don't ask them to know everything about the guitar.

I show them only what they need to know in order to solve the problem in front of them, in order to get their heads around this complex task of playing the guitar.

I show them one easy pattern on the neck and a few simple techniques for making certain kinds of sounds. That's it. It takes about five minutes to give the entire explanation.

When the explanation's over, I turn on the portable sound system I travel with, start a song, and play along with it, using only the techniques I just taught them.

I show them a very simple way to do it and then show them how it can sound if I make it more involved, more complicated. It is the building blocks that are critical. And we do this in everything.

What you learn and how you learn it will be guided by your goals, by what you're trying to accomplish.

TAKEAWAY: Break down a problem into its component parts and you will solve it more quickly than expected.

Lesson 43
Listen to Your Own Helpful Hints

Problems are not stop signs, they are guidelines.

~ Robert H. Schuller

If you don't like something, change it. If you can't change it, change your attitude. Don't complain.

~ Maya Angelou

You may be realizing at this point in the book that, in so many ways, you hold the key to your own success.

It's up to you to explore your beliefs, decide your priorities, and set your goals.

It's up to you to get the right tools for the job, identify your prime time, manage your calendars, and decide how to use technology.

It's up to you to say no to people who are trying to take your time.

And, if you're going to be honest with yourself right now, you know very well when things aren't working. You remind yourself all the time:

- "I can never find my keys!"
- "That guy is always coming into my office to gossip!"
- "I always forget things when I go shopping!"
- "Chores take me longer than they should!"

Most of the time, after your internal voice screams this frustration, nothing changes. You find your keys and go to work; you waste time talking to the guy in your office because you don't have the nerve to ask him to leave; you go back to the store, wasting valuable time; you continue to do chores the same way as always.

You're glad you got past that moment of frustration and you're ok...until the next time it happens.

There are indicators all around informing you that either you don't have a system or that your system isn't working well enough. When you raise the issue in your mind, you've taken an important step, but that's not sufficient.

You have to stay with the thought long enough to realize that something needs to be done. And then do it.

It's time to challenge yourself: when you hear that voice again, pay attention to it. Decide that you're going to do things differently. Decide that you're going to put a tool, technique, or method in place to fix the problem. After all, doing the same thing over and over expecting a different result is insane.

The following are examples of helpful hints your brain gives you rather often, telling you that your system is inadequate and needs to be improved:

I can never find my _____.

I have no place to put _____ .

I am tired of _____ .

I can't _____ because of the clutter.

I am losing a lot of money on _____ .

The disorganization makes me feel _____.

These may seem to be small and inconsequential adjustments. They're not. They will help reduce stress and frustration and change your outlook on what's possible. They will get your brain out of the business of focusing on petty nuisances and give you more energy, willpower, and discipline to tackle more important challenges.

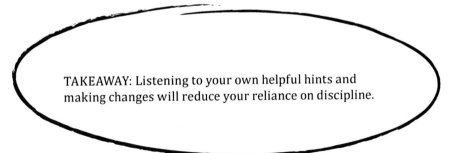

TAKEAWAY: Listening to your own helpful hints and making changes will reduce your reliance on discipline.

Learning to Say No

If you don't value your time, neither will others.

~ Kim Garst

The number one reason people fail in life is because they listen to their friends, family, and neighbors.

~ Napoleon Hill

When I was getting my Ph.D., I knew a professor who said no to a lot of things. It was a bit awkward to be on the receiving end of his no, but that wasn't his concern. When most other people would have said, "Yes," he simply said, "No." And that was it.

I soon realized it was no coincidence that he produced countless articles, received numerous grants, and won major awards in his field. He knew that saying yes to the wrong things would take him away from his goals.

Answer this very important question for yourself: Do I have a hard time saying no to people?

Saying yes — or the inability to say no — comes from a variety of places:

- You say yes to the wrong things in order to avoid something you're afraid of or don't want to face, like a difficult project or unpleasant task. You later use this distraction as an excuse for not facing your task head on.

- You grew up in a family, school, community, or church that valued saying yes to anyone who needed your help. To say no, then, might mean you're not honoring the values instilled in you growing up and can often result in feelings of guilt.

- You want to be liked, accepted, and part of the tribe. You don't want to come across as less than friendly. If you say no, you may be ostracized or exiled. You may be rejected and left alone.

- You don't have clear priorities and goals or a plan to reach them. When you don't have a plan to get to a desired goal or outcome, it's much easier to say yes to anything that comes along.

How does it feel at the end of the day to have given your time and energy away to other people and you have done nothing for yourself? You may begin to resent it, which then may affect so many other things in your life.

Like discipline in general, saying no is far easier when you have something important to say yes to.

1. Understand the Nature of the Beast

Do you know who you can say no to and who's a priority? If you say yes to everyone, then no one's a priority and you'll allow anyone and everyone take your time. Can you push most people, phone calls, and emails into your non-prime time?

2. Think in Advance

Most of us will allow interruptions if we have to decide at the moment of the interruption whether to allow it or not. Think in advance what you would say and how you would say it if someone wants your time. If you aren't sure how to do it, consult with a friend or colleague who's good at it.

3. Know Where You're Going

Successful people who get what they want are usually very good about knowing where they're going. They set themselves up for success by understanding their goals, why they're going after those goals, and the road ahead. Knowing where you're going reduces the temptation of saying yes when you really need to say no.

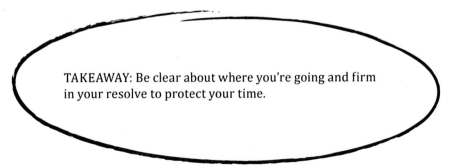

TAKEAWAY: Be clear about where you're going and firm in your resolve to protect your time.

Your Optimal Sleep Time

Sleep is that golden chain that ties health and our bodies together.

~ Thomas Dekker

To keep the body in good health is a duty... otherwise we shall not be able to keep our mind strong and clear.

~ Buddha

You may not think too readily about the connection between time management, sleep, and health. But, of course, if you're sick in bed or in the hospital, there goes your time management.

Sleep is one of the keys to having sufficient energy and discipline in getting what you want. You have to find what works for you. My preference is to go to sleep early. On a perfect night, I'm headed to bed at 8:00 pm, read, watch TV, or talk with my wife. Asleep by 9:00 pm and up around 4:00 am.

I work on most of my writing projects before the rest of the world wakes up. The books add to my accomplishments as well as the bottom line of my company and hopefully are useful to the readers.

When I talk about getting up at 4:00 am, my workshop audiences typically moan. And then I tell them about my wife. Jennifer hated to get up early. She was a champion sleeper on weekends, and had convinced herself she couldn't wake up early. Until she started writing a book.

She was so enthusiastic about the project that she looked forward to working on it.

On weekdays, Jenn would get up around 5:00 am and write for two hours before getting ready for work. Remember mastery? Slow and steady, day in and day out, will get you to your goal.

Yes, it is possible to wake up earlier. And if you think it's not, or you're convinced you can't, here are some ideas to try:

- Make small changes. Instead of convincing yourself you can't wake up an hour earlier each day, get up 15 minutes during the first week of your transition. Add more time in the second week.

- Go to sleep earlier. This one is easy to fudge and requires discipline. Set a specific time to be in bed. Turn off the television 30 minutes before your designated sleep time in order to start calming your mind.

- Break the snooze alarm habit. Put the alarm clock on the other side of the room, forcing yourself to get out of bed.

- Once you're out of bed, head straight to the bathroom. Do not return to bed. You'll be awake before you know it and moving toward your goals.

- Know what you will tackle first thing in the morning. Write your success list the night before. Choose your clothing the night before. Make your lunch the night before if you're taking it to work or school.

- When possible, use the buddy system. If you're waking up earlier in order to exercise, make a commitment to a friend or trainer to meet at a specific time.

- As with all other aspects of great time management, assess, assess, assess. Have you been successful in getting up earlier? If not, why not? What can you do differently?

When you know how to say no to requests for your time, put a system in place, and get clear about your goals, there will be enough time to sleep well *and* pursue your dreams.

If waking up earlier doesn't work for you, then organize your life so that you go to bed later and wake up later. Either way, you need to think in advance about how you might create the optimal time to go to bed and wake up to get the most out of your day while staying healthy.

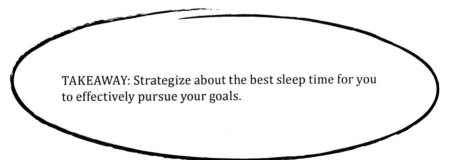

TAKEAWAY: Strategize about the best sleep time for you to effectively pursue your goals.

Lesson 46

E + R = O

The great majority of emotional distress
we experience results from how we think about
ourselves and our circumstances, rather than the
circumstances themselves.

~ Thom Rutledge

Between stimulus and response there is a space.
In that space is our power to choose our response.
In our response lies our growth and our freedom.

~ Viktor Frankl

As I wrote at the beginning, time management is really about self-management. It's about the choices you make in your life every day.

- You choose what to believe.
- You choose what to pursue.
- You choose to say yes or no to people.
- You choose how to spend your time.
- You choose how to manage your Self.

Whether you realize it or not, you get to choose how you respond to each and every event that happens. Events themselves are value neutral. They just "are."

The way you see events gives them their meaning. Much of your fear derives from your judgment of events that happen. Much of your time management is driven by what you choose to believe, what you choose to fear, and how you choose to act.

Typically, your fears, feelings, experiences, and judgments run deeper than the event itself. These might include anxiety about dying, fear of loss of control, fear of commitment, fear of rejection, and others.

The basic equation to help you remember this is E + R = O, where E is an Event that occurs, R is your Response to the Event, and O is the Outcome you are getting in your life. What Outcomes are you getting? Are you getting the Outcomes you want? Are you living the life you want?

If you want to change the Outcomes, you have to change your Responses.

While there may be several or numerous factors influencing your Outcomes, your Response to the Event may be the only thing in your control, the only thing you can change. You can't change the Event after it happens. You can't change other people.

But you can change the way you look at the Event and you can change how you Respond to people.

Increasing your awareness helps expand the set of responses you have in your toolkit and improve your time management.

In the quote above, Viktor Frankl essentially is saying you should draw out your Response time to Events.

When you draw out your Response time, you can formulate a more thoughtful Response rather than reacting instantaneously.

When you know who you are and what you want, you can make better Responses and improve your Outcomes.

When you improve your Responses and your Outcomes, you change your life.

TAKEAWAY: You change the Outcomes you get in life by changing your Responses to Events.

Gridiron Greatness: Don and Jeff's Story

Perfection is not attainable, but if we chase perfection we can catch excellence.

~ Vince Lombardi

The will to win, the desire to succeed, the urge to reach your full potential...these are the keys that will unlock the door to personal excellence.

~ Confucius

In 1987, Syracuse University football quarterback, Don McPherson, had an undefeated season. He won the Maxwell Award, the Davey O'Brien National Quarterback Award, and finished second in the Heisman Trophy voting. In 2008, he was inducted into the NCAA College Football Hall of Fame.

By now, you know the broad brushstrokes of how Don accomplished these feats. He used all of the main ingredients discussed in this book: belief, vision, priorities, goals, a system, and well-developed routines.

He had discipline, driven by the clarity of his goal and his passion for the game.

I had the privilege to watch him practice when we attended the same high school. Don would stay on the field after football practice and drill over and over: fade back, pass, improve his technique, fade back, pass, improve his technique.

His father would sometimes come out to the field and toss balls to him, helping him on his technique.

It's no surprise that Don took our high school team to the state championship and won. He was clear about the goal, broke down the complexity of football into smaller, digestible parts, and went for it.

Don was also a track star, using the same tools and techniques he applied to football to lead our track team to major championships.

The other person who figured in Don's football workouts was a junior high student named Jeff Dingle. After school, Jeff would run down the field, retrieving the footballs Don threw.

No one asked Jeff to come out. No one forced him. No one paid him. He understood at that age that if he was going to be a star, he needed to do what a star did.

He went on to college at Villanova where he was a football star and a track star. After college, he became a successful businessman.

Like Don, Jeff's discipline came out of great clarity, the right tools for the job, and a passion for what he did.

Both Don and Jeff demonstrated that the tools and techniques I've been discussing are effective and replicable: They work over and over again. Most successful people will tell you that they used the same path to reach their success.

Now we're reminded of the spiritual side of time management. Like the Irish priest I mentioned at the beginning said, "You don't know the hour or the day." On September 11, 2001, Jeff was attending a business breakfast at a restaurant on the top floor of the World Trade Center.

While we can focus on the pain, the grief, and the despair of losing him at such a young age with a young family left behind, the fact of the matter is Jeff lived more in his 36 years than most people do in 86 years. **Who are you? What do you want? How are you going to get it?** Are you willing to Get the Nerve to follow the examples of Don and Jeff?

TAKEAWAY: Time management techniques work because they're not about time; they're about choices.

Part 5:

Going Forward

The 7 Habits of Highly Effective People

*The main thing is to keep the main thing
the main thing.*

~ Stephen Covey

*But until a person can say deeply and honestly,
'I am what I am today
because of the choices I made yesterday,'
that person cannot say, 'I choose otherwise.'*

~ Stephen Covey

In 1989, Stephen Covey published his personal growth classic, *The 7 Habits of Highly Effective People*. While it wasn't publicized as a time management guide, it is, in fact, that (and so much more).

You would do well to read the book, memorize the habits, and start living them the best you can. When I started integrating the 7 habits into my life, everything changed.

Here is a preview of the 7 habits:

Habit 1: Be Proactive

Take initiative in life by realizing your decisions are the primary determining factor for effectiveness in your life. Take responsibility for your choices and whatever victories or consequences that follow.

Habit 2: Begin with the End in Mind

Self-discover and clarify your character values and life goals. Envision the ideal characteristics for each of your various roles and relationships in life.

Habit 3: Put First Things First

Plan, prioritize, and execute your tasks based on importance rather than urgency. Evaluate whether your efforts exemplify your desired values, propel you toward goals, and enrich the roles and relationships you choose for yourself.

Habit 4: Think Win-Win

Genuinely strive for mutually beneficial solutions or agreements in your relationships. Value and respect people by understanding a "win" for all is ultimately a better long-term resolution than if only one person in the situation gets his way.

Habit 5: Seek First to Understand, Then to be Understood

Use empathetic listening to be genuinely influenced by a person, which compels them to reciprocate the listening and take an open mind to being influenced by you. This creates an atmosphere of caring, respect, and positive problem solving.

Habit 6: Synergize

Combine the strengths of people through positive teamwork, so as to achieve goals no one person could have done alone. Get the best performance out of a group of people through encouraging meaningful contribution, and modeling inspirational and supportive leadership.

Habit 7: Sharpen the Saw

Balance and renew your resources, energy, and health to create a sustainable, long-term, effective lifestyle.

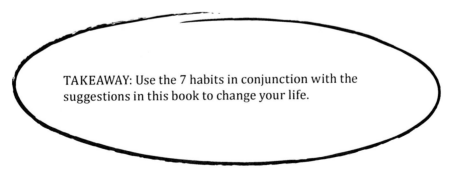

TAKEAWAY: Use the 7 habits in conjunction with the suggestions in this book to change your life.

Putting It All Together:
Frank's Story

Excellence is not a skill. It is an attitude.

~ Ralph Marston

Success is knowing your purpose in life, growing to reach your maximum potential, and sowing seeds that benefit others.

~ *John C. Maxwell*

My brother, Frank, did not set out to be recognized by President George H. W. Bush and receive the Volunteer Action Award. He didn't expect to be the recipient of President George W. Bush's Thousand Points of Light Award.

These accolades were made possible because Frank managed his Self.

He went to the Dominican Republic after graduating from dental school to fulfill our family philosophy of giving back to those less fortunate. Over time, he started recruiting American dentists and dental students to take the trip with him.

He has led the group for over thirty summers, easing the pain and discomfort of tens of thousands of people and providing millions of dollars' worth of dental care. One person's simple idea turned into a mission.

After his dental degree, he went on to earn a Master's as well as an MBA. He's spent his career working in dental school administration and teaching future generations of dentists.

He promised his teenage son he would travel to all of his soccer games even while he was studying for his MBA. Frank insisted that he and his son share a hotel room on the road, and they both studied together. Time management is serious business.

It's little coincidence that his son, as goalie, was an integral player when his high school soccer team won the state championship twice. Belief, visualization, priorities, goals, and excellence were established early in life.

His son went on to pursue his own priorities, traveling the world, learning to speak Chinese, and working for a global business consulting firm.

His daughter learned the lessons well, too. She was a voracious reader growing up, cultivating curiosity and insight at a young age. She received the first B ever in her academic career when she was in college. She'll finish medical school virtually debt-free.

Frank and his wife set up a parent-centric home. They were practiced at saying no to the kids because they understood that there were loftier goals than instant gratification. And they didn't have cable TV until a few years ago. The kids were not running the place.

Frank would tell his kids things like, "You can ask me any question you want before 7:00 pm. From 7:00-8:00, I will be in the garage doing woodworking. You're not allowed to bother me unless someone is bleeding or something is burning. I'll answer whatever other questions you have or things we need to take care of after 8:00 pm."

Perhaps there's a connection between that, the kids' reading habits, their financial success, and the strength of their family as a unit.

Frank became an accomplished woodworker and craftsman. He has also written several books and numerous academic articles. He's an experienced fisherman and blossoming guitar player.

By and large, Frank has spent his life saying yes to the right things and no to the wrong things and has instilled that habit in his kids.

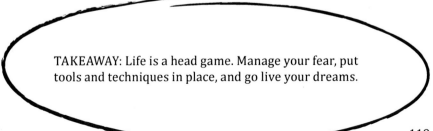

TAKEAWAY: Life is a head game. Manage your fear, put tools and techniques in place, and go live your dreams.

Everything is Connected

All is connected...no one thing can change by itself.

~ Paul Hawken

Success seems to be connected with action.
Successful people keep moving.
They make mistakes, but they don't quit.

~ Conrad Hilton

By now you know this one inescapable truth:

Your time management is connected to everything and
everything is connected to your time management.

When you manage your health, you're managing your time. Minimize your illnesses. Stay out of hospitals.

When you manage your exercise, you're managing your time. Keep exercising and stay active in order to regulate your weight, build strong muscles, and feel great.

When you manage your money, you're managing your time. You can reduce the probability of having to work a second and third job for the rest of your life and spend more time with your family.

When you manage your ego, you're managing your time. If you have to buy luxury items and a huge house to impress other people but don't have the income to do it, you will spend your valuable time trying to cover your bills and coping with the stress that will come with it.

When you manage your relationships, you're managing your time. Holding grudges, refusing to talk to people, keeping everything bottled up inside impacts your ability to focus, impacts your mastery, and impacts the outcomes you get in your life.

When you manage your staff, you're managing your time. A staff that is not confused about the mission, that doesn't walk on eggshells around the office, that feels secure in their environment will manage themselves better, be more productive, and help the organization thrive.

When you manage your learning, you're managing your time. Studying effectively and efficiently can create more opportunities and greater income for you.

When you manage your choices, you're managing your time. Don't give away your time too often to activities that have little or no meaning, little or no return.

When you manage your priorities and your goals, you're managing your time. Don't overextend yourself trying to be all things to all people.

I'm a big fan of the following unattributed quote:

> "Everything you do is based on the choices you make. It's not about your parents, your past relationships, your job, the economy, the weather, an argument, or your age that is to blame. You and only you are responsible for every decision and choice you make. Period."

That pretty much sums it up.

Your time management is about your self-management: your ability to manage your Self, to become your true Self, to stop hiding behind fears and excuses, and to make choices that support a happy, healthy, and productive life.

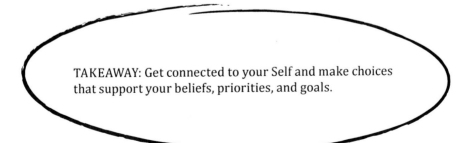

TAKEAWAY: Get connected to your Self and make choices that support your beliefs, priorities, and goals.

The Road Ahead

*This is the key to time management — to see the
value of every moment.*

~ Menachem Mendel Schneerson

*I know where I'm going and I know the truth, and
I don't have to be what you want me to be.
I'm free to be what I want.*

~ Muhammad Ali

It's no secret how successful people become successful, regardless of how you define success. They use tools and techniques like the ones outlined throughout this book. Their belief and their actions go hand in hand, each strengthening the other.

So often, we let others sway us from what we really want to do. We let them knock us off the path we really want to travel.

But more often than that, we're the ones who sabotage our own efforts. Regardless of how much we blame others, we are the ones who fail to manage our Selves.

Our time of excuses is over. We now have more than enough ways to improve our time management in order to get on the road to our dreams.

One bit of advice I can share with you as you contemplate the road ahead: find an accountability partner, a coach, or mentor to work with you. When done right, time management can be scary: It means facing fears, giving up excuses, hitting plateaus, and sometimes failing. You will run into frustrations and roadblocks; you'll try to bite off more than you can chew.

Having someone by your side whom you trust and has gone through this journey will make your steps so much easier to take. Together, you can define your goals, put a system in place, and understand when discipline is needed.

The key is small bites consistently over time.

Take the time to experiment, develop your own time management strategy, and do what's best for you — as long as it produces positive results.

Don't kid yourself that you're getting a lot done if you're simply being busy. Don't worry about what other people think of you; remember, people's opinion of you is none of your business.

I challenge you to consciously Decide how your life is going to be. I challenge you to Commit to managing yourself so that you can have the life you want. You have all of the tools you need to build an effective time management strategy — to Succeed.

So, before you close this book, write down the one thing about your current time management habit that you will change immediately. It may be simply getting a container for your keys or organizing your calendars. Pick one thing and do it.

It's possible you've been struggling for so long with your frustration and exhaustion. You may doubt that these time management techniques work. You don't have to take my word for it.

Re-read the stories about John, Kandy and Steve, Don and Jeff, and Frank. They are average people, like you and me, who took the basic time management — self-management — tools and put them to work. When they fell down, they didn't take it personally. They examined their process, got back up, and continued on.

You are more powerful than you imagine. You have the power to change your life. You hold the key to unlock every prison door you've created. Amazing things will happen when you do.

It all begins with you.

I would love to hear about your successes. You can reach me at drjoe@joeserio.com.

The Takeaways

Lesson 1   Time management is fundamentally about self-management.

Lesson 2   Your self-management honors the spiritual nature of your life.

Lesson 3   Increasing your self-awareness is the first step toward improving time management.

Lesson 4   Answer the three core questions to begin to clarify how you will best use your time.

Lesson 5   Understanding your fears and feelings is key to making lasting changes.

Lesson 6   It's time to change your perception and, hence, the reality of what you can handle.

Lesson 7   Get off your 'buts' and take charge of your destiny.

Lesson 8   Let go of perfect and strive to be your best, most excellent Self.

Lesson 9   There's less to be scared of than you think.

Lesson 10   Running your life based on what you think other people want is a trap.

Lesson 11   Moving forward requires courage, not the absence of fear.

Lesson 12   If John can do it, why not you?

Lesson 13   Belief in yourself is one of the cornerstones of effective goal setting.

Lesson 14   You will set the right goals and minimize distractions when you're clear about your priorities.

Lesson 15   You create twice, first in your mind and then in reality. See your future and then go get it.

Lesson 31   Make real forward progress by writing your success list instead of a to-do list.

Lesson 32   Your calendar is a key part of your system to track your time and manage activities.

Lesson 33   Strategize about how to use the phone to get the most out of your day.

Lesson 34   Be sure to control your email before it controls you.

Lesson 35   Use technology to make as many tasks, chores, and projects in your life as easy as possible.

Lesson 36   Use your screens to your advantage; don't throw away valuable time on countless hours of senseless viewing.

Lesson 37   You can do in 20 uninterrupted minutes what it takes to do in 60 interrupted minutes.

Lesson 38   Set yourself up so that your progress doesn't rely solely on discipline and willpower.

Lesson 39   Try, fail, improve. Try, fail, improve. That's the master's journey.

Lesson 40   Understand that staying on the plateau is a critical part of your process to reach mastery and success.

Lesson 41   Focusing on one task whenever possible makes for higher-quality work and less stress.

Lesson 42   Break down a problem into its component parts and you will solve it more quickly than expected.

Lesson 43   Listening to your own helpful hints and making changes will reduce your reliance on discipline.

Lesson 44   Be clear about where you're going and firm in your resolve to protect your time.

Lesson 45   Strategize about the best sleep time for you to effectively pursue your goals.

Acknowledgements

A special thanks to my wife, Jennifer, without whom this book series, our business, and the wonderful life we now enjoy together would not be possible.

This book would not be possible were it not for the countless conversations my brother, Frank, and I have had about time management and other related topics. More important, Frank modeled the fundamentals of time management over the years for me to observe in action. He has accomplished more than most of us might think possible.

Thanks to all who read the manuscript and offered feedback: Nancy Amato, Matt Bell, Bill Burt, Jim Comer, Edward Jackson, Jerry Kovar, Roxane Marek, Will Rutherford, Kim Schnurbush, Frank Serio, Tammy Spencer, Kristin Spivey, Kaia Tingley, and Ed Trevis.

Thanks to you for reading this book. I hope the suggestions discussed will help you in some small way as you discover your path ahead.

Our special gift to you:

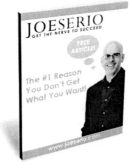

A FREE copy of our article,
"The #1 Reason You Don't Get What You Want"

Are you ready to have clarity around why you're struggling so you can start to make progress toward your goals?

This article will show you:

- The five myths about what's holding you back
- How these myths work against you
- Three powerful tools to make significant progress
- How your life will change once you master these tools

Stop waiting for something to change when you keep doing the same thing. Download this FREE ARTICLE and learn what you can do to have the life you want.

DOWNLOAD NOW at:

www.joeserio.com

Also in the *Get the Nerve™ Series*

Overcoming Fear:
50 Lessons on Being Bold and Living the Dream

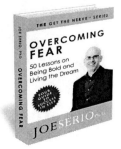

Take a good look at your life—is there something you would change, if you could? Why is it that you don't already have whatever it is you're longing for?

- A successful career you enjoy
- Loving, peaceful relationships
- The time and money to do what you want

Whether you know it or not, chances are fear has become an obstacle in your path to reaching your goals. Until you learn how to move past it, you'll continue to be stuck.

Stop fear in its tracks, and Get the Nerve™ to have the career, relationships, and lifestyle you want!

ORDER NOW!

www.joeserio.com

Also in the *Get the Nerve™ Series*

Public Speaking: 50 Lessons on Presenting Without Losing Your Cool

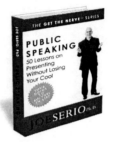

Does the thought of public speaking make you sick? Do you lie awake at night, weeks in advance of your event? Are you tired of living with the anxiety? Imagine turning all that around and feeling:

- Confident
- Calm
- Connected with your audience

Dr. Joe can help you manage your fear of public speaking so you can deliver killer presentations. In fact, as hard as it may be to believe, you can even learn to *enjoy* it.

Don't let your anxiety get in the way of your career!

ORDER NOW!

www.joeserio.com

Book Dr. Joe for your next training or event!

Dr. Joe is an expert in organizational behavior and can inspire your audience to see new possibilities and potential. He uses music and his own incredible life experiences to entertain and connect with your audience, enabling them to make unique connections between work and home so they can create improvements in *all* areas.

His most popular keynotes and trainings include:

- Overcoming Fear
- Time Management and Organizational Skills
- Positive Interaction with Difficult People
- Leadership and Legacy

To book Dr. Joe for your event, please visit:

www.joeserio.com

Or email us at:

drjoe@joeserio.com

Biography

Dr. Joe Serio is a popular and entertaining trainer and conference keynote speaker on leadership and change, time management and organizational skills, strategies for effective communication, and overcoming barriers to improved performance. He motivates and inspires his audiences while providing thought-provoking ideas.

Dr. Joe holds a Ph.D. in Criminal Justice with a specialization in Leadership and Organizational Behavior from Sam Houston State University (SHSU). As part of a unique internship program during graduate school at the University of Illinois at Chicago, Dr. Joe was the only American to work in the Organized Crime Control Department of the Soviet national police (MVD). During his stay in 1990-91, he conducted groundbreaking research on Soviet organized crime.

During this same period (1988-1993), Dr. Joe was the founding director of a summer study program at one of the five law schools in the People's Republic of China. The program included visits to Chinese prisons, neighborhood mediation committee meetings, courts, re-education through labor camps, and other criminal justice-related agencies.

In 1995-96, he worked as a Moscow-based consultant to the global corporate investigation and business intelligence firm, Kroll Associates. In 1997, he was named director of Kroll's Moscow office, where he managed a wide variety of investigations across the former Soviet Union and coordinated with Kroll offices around the world.

Dr. Joe is the author of the critically-acclaimed book, *Investigating the Russian Mafia*. He has delivered presentations to audiences in Russia, China, Canada, and the U.S. on Russian organized crime and security issues.

In the 1990s, he worked in Moscow as a media consultant to *The New York Times*, *The Washington Post*, CNN, BBC, and other media outlets. He helped produce three documentaries on Russian crime, including one inside Russian prisons, for the television program *Investigative Reports* on American cable channel A&E. He was also instrumental in producing the first-ever newspaper series on the Russian mafia. The eight-part series, "Glasnost Gangsters," appeared in the *Chicago Tribune* in 1991.

Dr. Joe also served for six years as Editor-in-Chief of the highly-regarded bi-monthly magazine, *Crime and Justice International*, which was produced at SHSU's Criminal Justice Center and distributed to more than 25 countries.

From 2013 to the present, Dr. Joe has been delivering conference keynote presentations to businesses, associations, and criminal justice agencies.

As a recorded musician, Dr. Serio occasionally brings music to his presentations, using harmonica and guitar to illustrate points pertaining to time management, organizational skills, and effective communication.

Follow him on...

Facebook: facebook.com/JoeSerioEnterprises

Twitter: twitter.com/JoeSerioSpeaks

YouTube: youtube.com/JoeSerioEnterprises

LinkedIn: linkedin.com/JoeSerioEnterprises

CPSIA information can be obtained
at www.ICGtesting.com
Printed in the USA
FFOW01n0941150716
25797FF